Classroom Management for All Teachers

11 Effective Plans

Classroom Management for All Teachers

11 Effective Plans

ENNIO CIPANI

California School of Professional Psychology

Merrill,
an imprint of Prentice Hall
Upper Saddle River, New Jersey   *Columbus, Ohio*

Library of Congress Cataloging-in-Publication Data

Cipani, Ennio

    Classroom management for all teachers : 11 effective plans / Ennio Cipani.
       p. cm.
    ISBN 0-13-520933-1
      1. Classroom management—United States—Handbooks, manuals, etc. 2.
School discipline—United States—Handbooks, manuals, etc.   I. Title.
    LB3013.C514   1998
    371.102′4—dc21

                                        97-27671
                                           CIP

Editor: Ann Castel Davis
Production Editor: Linda Hillis Bayma
Design Coordinator: Karrie M. Converse
Text Designer: STELLARViSIONs
Cover Designer: Susan Unger
Production Manager: Patricia A. Tonneman
Electronic Text Management: Marilyn Wilson Phelps, Matthew Williams, Karen L.
   Bretz, Tracey B. Ward
Director of Marketing: Kevin Flanagan
Marketing Manager: Suzanne Stanton
Advertising/Marketing Coordinator: Julie Shough

This book was set in Dutch 823 by Prentice Hall and was printed and bound by
Courier/Kendallville, Inc. The cover was printed by Phoenix Color Corp.

 © 1998 by Prentice-Hall, Inc.
Simon & Schuster/A Viacom Company
Upper Saddle River, New Jersey 07458

Printed in the United States of America

10 9 8 7 6 5 4 3

ISBN: 0-13-520933-1

Prentice-Hall International (UK) Limited, *London*
Prentice-Hall of Australia Pty. Limited, *Sydney*
Prentice-Hall of Canada, Inc., *Toronto*
Prentice-Hall Hispanoamericana, S. A., *Mexico*
Prentice-Hall of India Private Limited, *New Delhi*
Prentice-Hall of Japan, Inc., *Tokyo*
Simon & Schuster Asia Pte. Ltd., *Singapore*
Editora Prentice-Hall do Brasil, Ltda., *Rio de Janeiro*

About the Author

Ennio Cipani is a full professor in the ecosystemic child clinical psychology program at the California School of Professional Psychology. Prior to this position, he spent 12 years at the University of the Pacific as a member of the teaching faculty in the department of special education, the last 3 years being the department chair. He graduated from Florida State University with a Ph.D. in educational psychology. He has published many articles, chapters, and books on child behavior management, including *Noncompliance: Four Strategies That Work* and *Disruptive Behavior*. He has developed his own system of behavioral assessment entitled the "Cipani Behavioral Assessment and Diagnostic (C-BAD) System." He is a licensed psychologist in California with a private practice, primarily training the parents and teachers of referred children in a specific, individually tailored management plan for the child(ren) with severe behavior problems in the home and school.

Preface

Many personnel turn to behavioral plans and programs when a child's behavior has become extremely problematic. Certainly, these plans are well suited for extreme circumstances, to change behavior problems by developing more appropriate behavior in those children. The research base is replete with examples of validated management strategies. But one should not conclude that these plans are only of use in these "dire" circumstances. I have often heard teachers say, "Oh, his behavior isn't bad enough to warrant a behavioral plan." This equating of behavior plans as only appropriate for severe levels of problem behaviors has been perpetuated by misguided people, and nothing could be further from the truth!

Instead, one should look at the use of these plans as good prevention. An effective classwide behavior management system will probably prevent small problems from becoming bigger problems, and moderate-size problems from creating a disaster. Systematic behavior management is not just for treatment, it is good prevention.

CONTENTS OF THIS TEXT

This teacher manual presents user-friendly information on 11 classroom management plans for use with individual children or entire classes.

Management plans are detailed for two common problem areas:

1. Student on-task and assignment completion problems.

2. Student disruptive behavior and rule violations.

Part 1 contains five management plans designed to increase student on-task behavior or a student's completion of class assignments, or both. This problem area is addressed first because of its importance. If a teacher can develop a strategy that increases the student's engagement in task materials and teacher-presented instruction, other behavior problems will often greatly decrease. When children are *"engaged"* in tasks and academic instruction, there is less opportunity to engage in other (unacceptable) behavior. It is strongly recommended that teachers become familiar with the plans contained in Part 1 and apply them frequently, both to prevent potential problems and to solve current problem behaviors.

Disruptive behavior and rule violations are addressed in Part 2. Most behavioral plans described in this section for dealing with a student's disruptive behavior also add a strategy from Part 1 to increase on-task behavior or task completion. For long-term results, it is recommended that disruptive behavior be addressed in this dual fashion: Design a plan for dealing with the disruptive behavior as well as a concurrent plan for reinforcing appropriate student on-task behavior.

PRESENTATION FORMAT OF EACH MANAGEMENT PLAN

A uniform format is used in this manual to present each classroom management plan:

1. Brief description of plan

2. Terms

3. Apparatus

4. Baseline measurement

5. Procedures

6. How it works

7. Additional considerations

8. Hypothetical cases

9. Forms

WHO CAN USE THIS MANUAL?

This manual is well suited for current and prospective teachers, as both a resource and preservice teaching tool. It provides in-depth coverage of specific classroom behavioral management plans for individual students as well as systems for entire classrooms. It is written in a nontechnical style, free of most "behavioral" jargon. One need not have extensive training in behavior therapy or learning theory to understand how to apply any of the techniques presented in this manual in their basic form. Obviously, developing variations of these techniques for unique circumstances may require additional training through courses and field supervision.

This teacher's manual is not designed to be a primary text for a course. It lacks a broad development of theory or child behavior, basic principles of learning, and human development. It is not intended to replace this information, but rather to act in concert with a primary textbook in classroom management and human development or learning. Its utility is in providing the user with some strategies for dealing with two sets of common problems found in elementary and secondary classrooms. It therefore serves as an often-needed bridge from theory to practice.

Its use in preservice education would provide students with specific applications for problem areas that confront teachers. This manual would be an appropriate supplemental text in the following four areas: (1) general and special education classroom management, (2) behavior management, (3) educational psychology, and (4) mainstreaming. For professors teaching classroom management courses, the section on on-task behavior and assignment completion problems can be used as a supplement to the primary text. Students in this class can acquire knowledge of five strategies to use for children who have on-task or assignment completion problems.

Unlike traditional classroom management texts, this manual provides *detailed* explanations of specific strategies and their implementation. As part of the class, the teacher may ask the students to select one or several techniques and, using the forms at the end of each chapter, write a Teacher Designated Plan for a hypothetical student or class.

Courses in behavior management can use this resource to supplement the primary text. Each section provides detailed programs for a variety of behavior problems found in the class. The instructor could begin by teaching management plans that address on-task and assignment-completion problems (Part 1), followed by a section that delineates classroom management plans for disruptive behavior (Part 2). This manual provides an excellent backup to traditional texts used in behavior management, because it fills in the holes left when specific techniques are addressed in only a page or two in traditional texts. Again, the forms provided at the end of each chapter will make this manual valuable to any prospective or current teacher and their professional library.

School psychologists can also benefit from this manual, and its use in an educational psychology course would be appropriate. School psychologists are often asked to consult on cases in general and special education involving disruptive behavior, making Part 2 a valuable resource for them.

A final area of preservice course work for which this manual is appropriate is a course typically called "mainstreaming." Each year, students who plan to teach in general as well as special education take a course exposing them to children with disabilities. This course can also be referred to as "introduction to special education." The primary text for this type of class usually provides little or no information about specific classroom management strategies. Yet many general education teachers will be faced with behavioral problems in children both with and without disabilities, for which this manual could provide specific suggestions. The professor could augment these classes by selecting one to three techniques from both parts of the manual to present in detail. Given the nature of these introductory classes, the focus might be on the design of management plans for individual children who are experiencing difficulty staying on-task or engaging in disruptive behavior in inclusive settings.

ACKNOWLEDGMENTS

I wish to thank the following reviewers for their useful comments and understanding of the scope and intention of this material: Karen Lee Alexander, Bemidji State University; Paul Beare, Moorhead State University; Jim Burns, The College of St. Rose; Diane Connell, Notre Dame College, Manchester, New Hampshire; Robert J. Evans, Marshall University; Christine C. Givner, California State University, Los Angeles; Kathleen Gruenhagen, North Georgia College; Mary LaCoste, Xavier University of New Orleans; Tom McFarland, Lewis-Clark State College; Martha J. Meyer, Butler University; Nikki Murdick, Southeast Missouri State University; and Peggy Perkins, University of Nevada, Las Vegas.

Contents

PART 2

Plans for Reducing or Eliminating Disruptive and Rule-Violation Behavior 79

PART 1

Plans for Keeping On-Task and Completing Assignments

INTRODUCTION

What Is On-Task Behavior?

On-task behavior has been studied in many empirical investigations (Kazdin & Bootzin, 1972; Kazdin & Klock, 1973; Wolery, Bailey, & Sugai, 1988). It is commonly defined as the student attending to work or teacher-presented instruction. Specifically, in a paper-and-pencil task or a reading task, children are considered on-task if they are engaged in either reading the materials ("face-to-book" orientation), or writing or looking at the paper. Examples of *off-task behavior* would involve getting out of their seat, staring at the ceiling or floor, talking to a friend, and so on. In the case of teacher oral presentations, the child is expected to be looking in the teacher's direction. Therefore any instances in which the child is not looking at the teacher are considered off-task.

While measures of on-task behavior may not be ideal (from the standpoint of measuring a child's attention), they are acceptable approximations of a child's level of attention. Obviously one cannot get inside the child's mind to see if the information is being received and processed. It is possible that a child may be looking at the teacher, but not attending and processing information. However many studies have demonstrated a high correlation between attending (on-task) and work completion (Cohen & Close, 1975; Jackson, 1979; Schipp, Baker, & Cuvo, 1980).

What Constitutes On-Task and Assignment Completion?

In many classes, on-task rates during class assignments or lectures vary from student to student. Some students are engaged in their assignments at a high level, others complete part of their work, and some children are infrequently engaged in their assignment (which produces minimal completion of their assignment).

Children who generate high levels of on-task behavior are generally those who complete the assignments. The converse also is generally true. Children who have performance problems are those who have low rates of work completion or high rates of inaccurate performance of the assignments, or both. They also demonstrate lower rates of on-task behavior.

When a child is capable of performing an assignment, but does not perform the work accurately or on time because of lack of motivation, a strategy to deal with this performance problem may be needed. The five management plans presented in Part 1 of this text are well suited for these children. However, some children may also demonstrate performance problems that are the result of their lack of ability with the work (e.g., they do not understand the material). The management plans presented here would not address these children's needs; other teaching techniques would need to be considered.

The Ramifications of On-Task and Assignment Completion Problems

The long-term effects of a child's inability to stay on-task and complete assignments can range from poor grades and low self-esteem to skill deficits in the academic content areas. Obviously children who have adequate to good study habits profit more from the classroom learning environment than do students who have difficulty attending to teacher instruction or completing class or home assignments. Furthermore, children who are consistently off-task often engage in disruptive behavior, which disturbs the learning environment for themselves and others.

Dealing with On-Task and Performance Problems

Teachers use several common strategies to deal with on-task problems and difficulty in completing assignments. In many cases, teachers will mildly admonish children who are not engaged in the reading or written assignments. For example, a child may start daydreaming and the teacher might comment, "Sarah, you need to get back to reading your assignment and not daydream so much." In many circumstances the child attends to this directive (to engage in reading) at that point in time, and the teacher immediately attends to another child or task. However this admonishment does not produce greater attention to the task in the long run for many children. Often, the teacher finds that children who have trouble remaining on-task require more and more directives to stay engaged in the material.

A second strategy that has received empirical attention is to praise children when they are on-task (Kazdin & Klock, 1973; Madsen, Becker, & Thomas, 1968; Walker, Hops, & Fiegenbaum, 1976). The teacher spots several children who are doing their work and draws attention to them in the following manner, "I like the way Bobby, Sharon, Rhonda, and Bill are doing their work. It is nice to see those students behaving well in class and learning the material." While praise has been shown to be effective in increasing on-task behavior, its use has to be extremely systematic and frequent to effect changes in children's on-task behavior. Very often the teacher monitors the class less frequently as time goes by, and subsequently the level of praise for such behavior goes down dramatically. With this infrequent attention to the children's on-task behavior, praise (*by itself*) becomes an ineffective strategy.

Effective Strategies for On-Task and Performance Problems

The behavioral plans presented in Part 1 of this text address two major requirements for increasing on-task and accurate assignment completion: (1) the plan systematically provides for monitoring on-task behavior and subsequent reinforcing of this behavior when it does occur, and (2) the plan provides for systematic monitoring of accurately completed assignments and reinforcement when the child completes class assignments.

In the case of the first requirement, several of the management strategies in this text require the teacher to monitor the students' behavior systematically as to whether the children are on-task. For example, in the "beeper system," the teacher is cued by a series of beeps to monitor on-task behavior across the entire class. Children who are on-task at the time of the beeps are given points. In the case of Grandma's Rule, individual students are monitored as to their in-seat performance. Grandma's Rule invokes a contingency between staying in-seat for a relatively short time (low probability behavior) and getting out-of-seat (high probability behavior). Staying in-seat for a designated period of time results in the child being allowed to leave her seat. This can be an extremely effective tool for teaching young children to gradually learn how to stay in their seat and do their work.

Monitoring and rewarding accurate assignment completion is another method one can use to ensure that children are attending to the task. In the Beat the Clock game, students are given a time limit for finishing an assignment, and their completion of assignments is gauged in direct proportion to the time limit designated. If the children finish within the time, they are given points or earn extra time off from work (the "break card" plan).

Another way to increase attending and on-task behavior involves creating more interesting instructional formats. In the "response card" program (Narayan, Heward, Gardner, Courson, & Omness, 1990), the teacher presents a limited amount of information and then "tests" the children's comprehension using a dry erase board. Because each child will be asked to respond to questions frequently, attention and on-task behavior will increase (Narayan, et al., 1990).

The following list delineates the five management plans presented in this part and their application as relevant for individual student or class-wide applications.

Management Plan	Individual	Classwide
Beeper System	X	X
Grandma's Rule	X	
Break Cards	X	X
Response Cards		X
Beat the Clock	X	X

The Beeper System

BRIEF DESCRIPTION

The beeper system is an excellent management strategy for monitoring student on-task behavior (Erken & Henderson, 1989; Repp, Barton, & Brulle, 1983). The system uses random beeps (from a tape recorder) during one or more class periods. The beeps cue the teacher to scan the classroom and identify who is on task and who is off-task (Erken & Henderson, 1989; Henderson, Jenson, Erken, Davidsmeyer, & Lampe, 1986). Points are awarded to those students identified by the teacher as being on-task at the time of the beep. In some cases, students may be trained to accurately monitor their own behavior and record points if they were on-task.

At the end of the assignment or period, the number of points each student has earned is summed. Those students achieving or exceeding the behavior standard (usually set as a number of total earned points) trade in their points for a desired reinforcer. What they get and how much they get can be a function of how many points they earned that period. For example, students earning 80% of the total points could get 3 minutes of extra recess, whereas students who earn 95% of the total points would earn 5 extra minutes. A master chart keeps track of each child's points each time the beeper system is used. Self-monitoring children keep their own charts.

The beeper system provides random but frequent beeps in the beginning stage of implementation, to increase the chances of catching the children on-task. The number of beeps is gradually reduced as the children need less frequent monitoring to stay on-task. The beeper system can be used for one or a few children who have extremely low rates of on-task behavior as well as for an entire class.

TERMS

behavior standard   the number of points a child must earn to access reinforcement.

self-monitor   students determine individually if they are on-task at each beep and record the designated number of points earned.

APPARATUS

One piece of apparatus includes an audiotape with a series of beeps occurring at variable time intervals[1]. Each tape produces 1-second beeps for a designated period of time. Let's say the teacher uses the beeper system for a 45-minute class period. She wishes to start with 30 beeps within that time frame. She would purchase or develop several 45-minute audiotapes, with the time sequence of beeps different for each tape. Obviously if only one tape was used, students would quickly learn the pattern of beeps for

---

[1] Can be purchased from Erken Learning Center, 1904 Marin Drive, Santa Rosa, California 95405.

that tape (and then learn to go on-task selectively!). If six to nine tapes are developed, students would be hard pressed to memorize the patterns on all the tapes.

If audiotapes are not available, an oven timer can be used. The teacher designates a time interval in which the oven timer is to be set (e.g., between 10 and 40 seconds). The teacher sets the oven timer for a value between those two points (e.g., 10 and 40 seconds). When the timer goes off, the teacher scans the class for on-task behavior, notes who gets points, and then resets the timer for a value within those two points again. The process of setting the oven timer is repeated until the end of the period.

Another necessary item is the student point chart, which records the points each student has earned on the beeper system. Figure 1.1 is a sample student point chart that illustrates a 7-beep system for a 20-minute period for three students. The maximum number of points possible is 35. The number of points needed to earn 3 or 5 minutes of extra free time is 26 and 32 points, respectively.

The point total for each student across the 20-minute period is given in the far right column. The chart shows that J. L. and S. T. earned 3 minutes of extra free time (by earning 31 and 30 points respectively). R. V. earned only 14 points total, and therefore did not earn free time.

Finally, a beeper "point card" with point values should be made. When implementing the beeper system, it is wise to not provide the same number of points for each beep (otherwise students learn that if they have reached the standard early, they can "coast" for the rest of the period). The teacher should use a variety of point payoffs at each beep. The beeper card provides five to seven variations of points across the number of beeps, so the students never know which beeps produce large numbers of points. Figure 1.2 shows a sample beeper point card presenting five variations of a 5-beep system. Note that in Variation A a 10-point payoff occurs on the 5th beep. One would not want the students to learn that the 5th beep on the tape always results in 10 points. Sometimes it results in 4 points (Variation E).

A Sample Student Point Chart: Beeper System

Time frame: <u>20 minutes</u>

Number of beeps: <u>7</u>

Total possible points: <u>35</u>

Total points needed for 3 minutes free time: <u>26</u>

Total points needed for 5 minutes free time: <u>32</u>

Student/Beep	1	2	3	4	5	6	7	Total Points
J. L.	3	0	6	2	5	10	5	31
R. V.	3	4	0	2	0	0	5	14
S. T.	3	4	6	2	0	10	5	30

FIGURE 1.1
A Sample Student Point Chart: The Beeper System

A Sample Beeper Point Card
(total possible points: 100)

Variation/Number of beeps	1	2	3	4	5
A	27	13	31	19	10
B	12	31	23	18	16
C	6	30	27	25	12
D	15	4	15	2	14
E	20	5	9	12	4

FIGURE 1.2
A Sample Beeper Point Card

BASELINE MEASUREMENT

Baseline measurement involves determining the frequency of a behavior before a systematic technique is introduced. Its primary function is to allow the teacher to determine a reasonable behavior standard to use in the initial implementation of the plan. A reasonable standard is neither too high nor too low. For example, if a child is on-task 40% to 60% of the time, a behavior standard of 90% would be too high. Conversely, a behavior standard of 20% is probably too easy. A reasonable standard would be somewhere between 40% and 60%.

Baseline measurement of on-task behavior for this system merely requires the teacher to implement the beeper system in a designated class period without specifying the standard or providing the ability to earn special reinforcers. The teacher monitors on-task behavior during each beep and assigns points to the students who are on task. If desired, the teacher can let the students know how many points they have earned at the end of the period, as a partial incentive to remain on-task. However, no reinforcers are available during the baseline measurement.

After collecting baseline measurements for 5 to 8 days, the teacher is able to establish the number of points the students must get to earn the reinforcer. This is done by examining the baseline data across all students and arriving at a reasonable standard. In some cases, only one standard will be set (e.g., 80% of the total points). If there are several low performers in the class who might not reach this standard, two or more standards can be set in a graded fashion (e.g., 60% of the total points earns 2 minutes, 80% earns 4 minutes).

PROCEDURES

1. Design or purchase beeper tapes or purchase oven timer (see apparatus section for design instructions).

2. Designate class period(s) in which beeper system will be used and the subsequent time frame (e.g., 40 minutes, 50 minutes).

3. Design student point chart (Form 1.1, versions A, B, and C) and beeper point card (Form 1.2). Specify the number of beeps to occur on the point chart. Design several variations of points for the sequence of beeps.

4. Collect baseline data using beeper system for 5 to 8 days, but do not provide a special reinforcer for getting points nor set a standard during baseline monitoring.

5. After collecting baseline data, calculate the number of points the students will need across the class period to achieve the standard. If necessary, a graded system of two or more standards can be used (e.g., 80% of total points produces 4 minutes of free time, 90% produces 8 minutes of free time).

6. Inform the class of the beeper system.

7. Implement the beeper system during one target class period initially, and appoint a chart manager each period (see additional considerations below) to record each student's points for each beep during the class period.

8. When the beep goes off, scan the class, call out those students who earn points (or if only a few are off-task call off those who do not earn points). Provide intermittent praise for on-task behavior in addition to point allocation.

9. After the points are distributed, continue teaching.

10. Repeat the process with each beep and at the end of the period total up the number of points for each student. Determine who reached the behavior standard needed for free time (or whatever reinforcement is being used) and deliver the reinforcement.

HOW IT WORKS

The beeper system allows the teacher to track on-task behavior without substantially disrupting the instructional system. With continued practice, most teachers who have used this system report eventually becoming comfortable with the system, particularly as the number of beeps is reduced. With frequent, unpredictable monitoring, and feedback to students as to whether they are on-task, student on-task behavior increases. As a result of the setting of the standard, and the availability of a reinforcer for achieving the standard, students become more motivated to stay on-task and earn the reinforcer.

ADDITIONAL CONSIDERATIONS

Appointing a Chart Manager

If the beeper system is implemented by the teacher, it is advisable for the teacher to appoint a chart manager from the class for each period. By removing the function of record-keeping, the teacher can proceed with instruction after scanning the class and assigning the points to students who are on-task. The chart manager records this data, then returns to the assignment. The chart manager should be a different student each period so that no one person is allowed to perform this duty each day. A different student can be selected each period as a special "treat."

Teaching Students to Self-Monitor

At some point teachers should consider having students monitor their own on-task behavior and record the points they have earned, with teacher spot checks for accurate monitoring (McLaughlin, 1983, 1984). The specifics of a self-monitoring program are the same as for one using a chart manager, except that each student has a separate recording sheet (see Form 1.1). With each beep, the students identify whether they are on-task and write down the number of points stated by the teacher. At the end, the points are totaled and reinforcement is delivered to students reaching the standard. To ensure student accuracy, the teacher can conduct random spot checks of the recording sheets.

Low Performers

In some cases, low performers may not achieve the standard necessary for reinforcement. In this case, a lower behavior standard might be deployed for those students. Consider the following hypothetical data recorded over an 8-day period (percentage of total points a child earned) as a case of selecting an alternate standard for initial low performers:

J. F.'s Data

80%–100%	ll
60%–80%	llll
40%–60%	ll
below 40%	l

J. F. earned 80% or more of the total points on only one day, but earned more than 60% on 5 days. Therefore 60% might be selected as an initial standard for J. F. As J. F. achieves this standard regularly (8 out of 10 days), the standard is increased (e.g., 70%).

Another adaptation for low performers is to reduce the length of the time they are on the beeper system. For example, a 45-minute period for the class on the beeper system might be shortened for the low performers to the first 25 minutes. The low performers would not use the system for the remaining 20 minutes. Again, as they become adept at remaining on-task, the length of time they are on the beeper system is increased.

Finally, the number of beeps might be increased to allow the teacher more of an opportunity to catch the low-performing children on-task. Therefore, low performers might be on a separate tape (with different intervals between beeps) from the rest of the class, to allow for a greater number of beeps.

Increasing the Behavior Standard

Particularly when a standard has been set lower than the desirable goal for on-task behavior, the teacher should consider progressively increasing the standard. This is done with the aid of data.

For example, after 2 weeks of implementing the beeper system, the teacher may find that all students in the class have achieved the behavior standard of 65 (out of 100 points) on 8 of the 10 days in which the beeper system was implemented for a class period. She might then increase the behavior standard to 70 points needed to earn the reinforcement. If in the next 2 to 3 weeks, students reliably achieve or exceed this level, the teacher can again increase the standard by a few points (e.g., to 73). This process continues until the teacher is satisfied with the standard of on-task behavior, and the students are able to reliably achieve or exceed the standard.

Gradually Reducing the "Density" of Beeps

In the initial implementation of the beeper system, the density of beeps is great, to catch the children on-task more frequently. Once the children begin responding to the system, with increased on-task levels, the teacher can gradually and systematically reduce the number of beeps (see Form 1.3). The following suggested density of beeps and phases could be adapted by the teacher:

Phase I (initial implementation)	30 beeps
Phase II	25 beeps
Phase III	20 beeps
Phase IV	15 beeps
Phase V	10 beeps
Phase VI	5 beeps
Phase VII	3 beeps

With this progressive reduction of beeps, the teacher would begin at Phase I (or Phase II in a shorter time period). She would implement the next phase of beeps once the students increased their on-task behavior to a desirable level. If this level is maintained for 2 to 3 weeks, the teacher goes to the next phase. This progressive reduction continues, contingent on student performance remaining at high levels, until the teacher reaches Phase VI or VII.

A "Graded" System for Earning Reinforcement

In some cases, it might be wise to have two sets of behavior standards, a high one and a low one. The high standard, such as 90 points out of 100, might provide 5 minutes of extra video time on Friday. However to ensure that students don't give up once they have figured out they can't possibly get 90 points (after being off-task for a couple of beeps) a low standard might be set at 75 points, allowing students to earn 2 minutes of extra video time. By using such a graded system, you can keep students motivated even during sessions in which they have a couple of instances of off-task behavior.

◆ HYPOTHETICAL EXAMPLE

Two Low-Performing Target Students

Mr. Johanson is considering using the beeper system for two students in his sixth-grade class who have unacceptable levels of on-task behavior. He estimates that their on-task behavior on some days is less than 20%. He purchases an oven timer and decides to use the beeper system during the 9–10 A.M. class period. He divides the one-hour period into two 20-minute periods (with a 10-minute break in between). He wants to have 10 beeps occur during each 20-minute period, meaning the oven timer will have to ring every 2 minutes on the average. He therefore sets up five patterns of 10 beeps for a 20-minute period, with each beep occurring at a specific point in the 20-minute period.

To determine the initial behavior standard, he collects baseline data on the two students for 5 days. He establishes a 50-point maximum possible number of points for a 20-minute period. The baseline data indicate that Student No. 1 ranges from a low of 5 points to a high of 25 points, with a mean of 16. Student No. 2 has a low of 5 and a high of 30, with a mean of 20. Mr. Johanson decides to set one standard for both students because they are fairly similar in their average rate of on-task behavior. The behavior standard is the following: If the students earn 15 points, they get 5 minutes of an alternate preferred activity at the end of the 20-minute time frame. If they earn 20 points, they get 10 minutes of an alternate activity after the 20-minute time frame. If they do not earn either 5 or 10 minutes, they will continue working until the next time frame. Therefore, the students may work for 20 minutes and then have a 10-minute alternate in-seat activity period before working for another 20 minutes followed by another 10 minutes of alternate activity (if they earn the maximum possible).

Mr. Johanson informs the students of the beeper system, how it works, and how many points they have to accumulate in the 20-minute period to earn 5 or 10 minutes of an alternate activity. He posts a form with the specific details (see Form 1.5). He sets the beeper point card in the top drawer next to the oven timer and implements the system. When the timer goes off he immediately observes the two target students and records the points each has earned. He resets the oven timer for another interval and continues teaching, working with students who need help. At the end of the 20-minute period when all the 10 beeps have occurred and points have been recorded, he determines immediately which of the two students (or both) has earned an alternate activity. The student who has earned 10 minutes can stop at that point and engage in an alternate in-seat activity. If the student earned only 5 minutes, she or he must continue working 5 more minutes before engaging in the more preferred alternate activity. If the students do not earn any alternate-activity time, they must continue working for the entire 10-minute time period before the next 20-minute work period.

After two weeks of implementation, Mr. Johanson is pleased with the results. Both students have done so well that the behavior standard is now 35 out of 50 points to earn 5 minutes of free time and 45 points to earn 10 minutes. Both students in the past several days have earned at least 5 minutes of free time at every opportunity.

FORMS

Notes

FORM 1.1
(VERSION A)

Student Self-Management Chart: 10 Beeps

Student's Name _____

Date _____   Period _____   Total possible points _____   Number of points needed _____

Beeps   Points awarded

1

2

3

4

5

6

7

8

9

10

Total

FORM 1.1
(VERSION B)

Student Self-Management Chart: 15 Beeps

Student's Name _____

Date _____   Period _____   Total possible points _____   Number of points needed _____

Beeps	Points awarded
1	
2	
3	
4	
5	
6	
7	
8	
9	
10	
11	
12	
13	
14	
15	
Total	

FORM 1.1
(VERSION C)

Student Self-Management Chart: 20 Beeps

Student's Name _____

Date _____   Period _____   Total possible points _____   Number of points needed _____

Beeps	Points awarded
1	
2	
3	
4	
5	
6	
7	
8	
9	
10	
11	
12	
13	
14	
15	
16	
17	
18	
19	
20	
Total	

FORM 1.2

Beeper Card

100 points possible—4 variations of points across 10 beeps

	Number of beeps									
	1	2	3	4	5	6	7	8	9	10
Variation A	5	15	6	9	21	7	2	18	12	5
Variation B	9	6	21	15	5	12	5	7	2	18
Variation C	13	13	5	14	8	7	1	19	12	8
Variation D	7	12	9	8	20	24	3	9	4	4

FORM 1.3

Beeper System: Teacher Designated Plan

Target class:

On-task behavior(s):

Baseline data across students in class for five sessions (average percentage of on-task behavior across all students):

(1) _____

(2) _____

(3) _____

(4) _____

(5) _____

Standard for earning reinforcement (number of points needed): _____

Criteria for adjusting time standard up: _____

Criteria for adjusting time standard down: _____

Number of initial beeps: _____

Criteria for decreasing number of beeps: _____

Parental consent (if needed): _____

Administrator signature (if needed): _____

FORM 1.4

Progress Summary

Date: _____

Class: _____

Baseline rates of on-task behavior (across class): _____

Current rate (across class): _____

Progress toward objective: Yes   No

Maintain current plan: Yes   No

Revise current plan: Yes   No

FORM 1.5

Beeper System: Class Posting of Rules

Rule: Remain in Your Seat and Engaged in Your Work

Total number of points possible: _____

Number of points needed: _____

Class periods/time for beeper system: _____

Grandma's Rule for Increasing In-Seat Behavior

BRIEF DESCRIPTION

Some children, especially younger children, have difficulty remaining in their seat for relatively long periods of time. In early elementary grades, some classroom activities require the child to sit for 10, 20, or even 30 minutes. Children who have the ability to remain in their seats for only a few minutes at a time obviously would have difficulty with these activities. Teachers report that there are still many children who have difficulty sitting (and attending) for a period of time, even after being referred for medication, counseling, and so on.

The management plan presented in this chapter gradually increases in-seat behavior using a principle inherent in Grandma's Rule (Premack, 1965). Grandma's Rule goes something like this: "You don't get your dessert until you eat your vegetables." The rule describes a basic relationship between an undesirable event (eating vegetables) and a preferred event (eating dessert). This basic relationship between undesirable events and preferred events can be used to increase a child's in-seat behavior in classrooms. The teacher would require the child to be in-seat for a short designated period of time. If the child stays in-seat for this time period, the teacher would allow the child to get out of his seat for some period of time. In other words, the child would earn out-of-seat time for being in-seat for a certain amount of time.

To use Grandma's Rule to increase in-seat behavior, the teacher identifies the child's current ability to remain in-seat. He collects baseline data on the rate of out-of-seat occurrences during a designated class period. If the child gets out of his seat five times in a 20-minute period, the average interval of in-seat behavior can be computed (see Form 2.1). The teacher divides the number of times the child gets out of his seat (5) into the length of the period (20). This would yield the *average* interval of in-seat behavior. (In this case the average interval would be 4 minutes.)

With this average interval of in-seat behavior identified, a behavior standard is set. Usually the teacher can use this average length as the standard (see Form 2.2), or something close to this value. The behavioral plan requires the child to be in his seat for that period of time to earn several minutes of out-of-seat time *right after that interval*. If the child stays in his seat for 4 minutes, he immediately gets 4 minutes of out-of-seat time. However, if the child gets up before the 4-minute interval, he is brought back to his seat and the timer is reset to 4 minutes. When the child reliably achieves the standard, the teacher can gradually increase the in-seat interval required. Concurrently, the teacher also begins decreasing the out-of-seat time that is earned.

TERMS

Premack Principle   the idea that a behavior of high probability can be used to reinforce a behavior of lower probability (Premack, 1965).

average interval of in-seat behavior   the average (mean) length of time children are able to stay in their seats over a period of time. It is calculated by dividing the length of the period (e.g., 60 minutes) by the number of times the child gets out of the seat (e.g., 12), which would yield a 5-minute average interval of in-seat behavior.

in-seat standard   the length of time the child must remain in-seat (continuously) to be allowed out-of-seat for a designated period of time.

APPARATUS

The apparatus needed for this program is an oven timer that can be reset. It can be placed on the child's desk or on the teacher's desk.

BASELINE MEASUREMENT

The teacher needs to determine the average length of in-seat behavior for the target child. As delineated above, he must record the frequency of out-of-seat behavior during a specific designated period (e.g., 10-11 A.M.). He then divides the frequency of out-of-seat behavior into the length of time (e.g., 10 out-of-seat occurrences in 60 minutes yields an average in-seat interval of 6 minutes). The teacher immediately sits the child back in the seat when he gets up, to compute an accurate estimate of the in-seat interval. The teacher does this for a 6- to 8-day baseline period. A chart like the one in Figure 2.1 will help the teacher collect and record this data.

Child Sarah K.   Time Period 10 to 11 A.M.

Date	Number of Out-of-Seat Occurrences	Total	Length of Period	Avg. In-Seat Interval
1. 3/5	⊢⊢⊢⊢ I	6	24	4 min
2. 3/8	⊢⊢⊢⊢ IIII	9	27	3 min
3. 3/9	⊢⊢⊢⊢	5	20	4 min
4. 3/10	⊢⊢⊢⊢ ⊢⊢⊢⊢	10	25	2.5 min
5. 3/10	⊢⊢⊢⊢ I	6	30	5 min
6. 3/11	⊢⊢⊢⊢ III	8	24	3 min
7.				
8.				

FIGURE 2.1
Baseline of In-Seat Interval

PROCEDURES

1. Identify target child.

2. Collect 6 to 8 days of baseline data in the target class period(s).

3. Set the initial in-seat standard by computing the average interval of in-seat behavior across the designated time period (i.e., the number of out-of-seat occurrences divided into the duration of the class period). Use this value to determine the initial in-seat standard, setting an oven timer for that amount.

4. Tell the child that he must remain in-seat for the length of time that the oven timer is set (see Form 2.3).

5. If the child gets out of seat before the oven timer rings, redirect the child back to his seat and *reset* the timer for the full in-seat standard time period.

6. If the child achieves the in-seat standard, praise the child, and allow the child a designated period of time to be out of seat (usually a few minutes). Repeat this process of setting an in-seat interval, and giving the child out-of-seat time when he is successful.

7. Once the child conforms regularly to the initial in-seat standard for several days in a row, increase the in-seat interval by a minute or two (see Form 2.4).

8. Continue adjusting the in-seat standard while gradually decreasing the earned out-of-seat time period until the in-seat interval reaches the desired goal (e.g., 20 minutes), depending on the child's age or grade level.

HOW IT WORKS

A specific plan is needed for many children entering the elementary grades who have not acquired the skill of sitting in a seat for a long period of time. Often, teacher efforts to develop this skill fail, because their expected standard far exceeds the child's ability. For example, children who generally cannot sit for longer than 3 to 5 minutes are required to sit continuously for 25 minutes during a class assignment to receive reinforcement. They never acquire the ability to sit continuously for a designated period of time, making teaching them a more difficult proposition as they get older. In-seat behavior should be addressed early in the child's educational life. This individual management plan can be tailored to teach each child how to remain in-seat for longer and longer periods of time.

Using out-of-seat time to reinforce children for staying in their seats for a designated period of time gives this program its "power" to gradually develop in-seat behavior. As children stay in their seats for a designated period of time, being out-of-seat becomes a more potent reinforcer, and thus a powerful reward for staying in-seat. As the child becomes competent at remaining in-seat, even for a relatively short period of time (e.g., 4 minutes), the teacher can develop the desired level of in-seat capability (e.g., 25 minutes) by gradually increasing the in-seat standard (from 4 to 6 minutes, then to 8 minutes, and so on).

ADDITIONAL CONSIDERATIONS

Implementing the Program with One Student at a Time

Because this program requires intensive intervention and supervision by the teacher, the teacher may want to institute this program with only one child at a time. Therefore, if several children in the class lack skill staying in their seat, consider implementing it with only one or possibly two children at a time. To attempt to implement this individualized program across many children in a class would be extremely time consuming, and additional personnel and resources would probably be needed. However, the simplicity of this program lends itself well to being implemented by non-certificated personnel, in inclusive environments.

◆ HYPOTHETICAL EXAMPLE

Increasing In-Seat Behavior in a Fourth-Grade Student

Mr. Jang is concerned about Juan's inability to remain in his seat to work on his class assignments. Juan is constantly getting out of his seat and Mr. Jang continually has to redirect Juan back to his seat. He considers implementing Grandma's Rule to increase in-seat behavior with Juan and collects 4 days of baseline data in 2 class periods: one between 9 and 10 A.M. and the other, between 10 and 11 A.M. Mr. Jang counts the frequency of Juan's out-of-seat behavior and divides this number into 60 minutes to come up with an average interval for that period of in-seat behavior. The following interval lengths were obtained:

	9 A.M. Class	10 A.M. Class
Mon.	7 mins.	3 mins.
Tue.	10 mins.	2 mins.
Wed.	10 mins.	3 mins.
Thu.	12 mins.	1 min.

As a result of the baseline data Mr. Jang sets the in-seat standard (for the 9 A.M. class) at 10 minutes and the 10 A.M. class at 2 minutes. Mr. Jang hopes that Juan eventually will be able to stay in-seat for 25 to 30 minutes in both classes. If Juan stays in his seat for 10 minutes in the 9 A.M. class, as identified by an oven timer, he is allowed to get up and stretch his legs for 3 minutes, provided he does not disrupt the class. If Juan gets out of his seat before that time, he is immediately redirected back to his seat and the oven timer is reset for 10 minutes.

The same procedure holds true from 10 to 11 A.M., except that Juan must sit for 2 minutes. After 2 weeks of implementation of the plan, Juan missed only two opportunities to earn reinforcement (i.e., the timer had to be reset) during the 9 to 10 A.M. time period, and five opportunities from 10 to 11 A.M. Based on this, Mr. Jang raised the behavior standard to 14 minutes from 9 to 10 A.M. and the behavior standard from 10 to 11 A.M. is adjusted to 5 minutes. Mr. Jang is confident that in time, Juan will be able to sit for the target goal of 20 minutes for both periods.

◆ HYPOTHETICAL EXAMPLE

Increasing Sitting During Story Time

Miss Haratio has identified several kindergarten students who are experiencing difficulty listening to a story for 10 minutes at a time. She decides to implement this program with each student individually. If this program is successful with the first child, she will implement the plan with the other two. Miss Haratio identifies that Tanicia gets up during story time about five times in a 10-minute period. That is a 2-minute average sitting time during story time.

All the children have carpet squares and are expected to sit in the carpet square while the teacher reads the story to the class. Miss Haratio informs Tanicia that a timer will be set for 2 minutes. If she can remain on the carpet square for 2 continuous minutes, she may then get up and stand by Miss Haratio for a short period of time. However if Tanicia gets up before the timer goes off, she is not allowed to stand next to Miss Haratio. Rather, she will be required to sit back on the carpet square for an additional 2 minutes. Within a month, Tanicia is able to sit at least 6 continuous minutes before getting up. Building on this success, the teacher plans to use it for the next two students who also need help in this area.

FORMS

2.1   Baseline Chart of In-Seat Interval

Allows teacher to calculate average in-seat interval over several days (can use this data sheet for data collection during Grandma's Rule). Sum tally marks, divide into length of time.

2.2   Monitoring Sheet for Grandma's Rule

Teacher posts this at child's desk, specifying the target goal and recording each time child was able to remain in-seat for the target interval length within the class period.

2.3   Rule Reminder for Student

Teacher posts this for student(s).

2.4   In-Seat Behavior: Teacher Designated Plan

Teacher uses for delineating specifics of Grandma's Rule management plan—to be used for I.E.P.'s.

2.5   Progress Summary

FORM 2.1

Baseline Chart of In-Seat Interval

Child: _____

Date	Number of Out-of-Seat Occurrences	Total	Length of Period	Avg. In-Seat Interval
1.				
2.				
3.				
4.				
5.				
6.				
7.				
8.				

FORM 2.2

Monitoring Sheet for Grandma's Rule

Child:_____

Date: _____

Period:_____

Target in-seat Interval: _____

_____

Tally number of times child meets in-seat standard above during the period:

Tally: _____   Total:_____

FORM 2.3

Rule Reminder for Child

Rule:

Stay in your seat until the timer goes off. Ask teacher to leave seat when timer goes off.

You have earned time off.

— FORM 2.4 —

In-Seat Behavior: Teacher Designated Plan

Child: _____

Target behavior(s): _____Continuous in-seat behavior_____

Designated class period(s): _____

Baseline data across five times/sessions (designate average interval):

Days   1._____

2._____

3._____

4._____

5._____

Initial in-seat standard (continuous in-seat interval): _____

Criteria for adjusting in-seat standard up: _____

Criteria for adjusting in-seat standard down: _____

Length of time child allowed out-of-seat (standard achieved): _____

Rules for out-of-seat time: _____

Parental consent (if needed): _____

Administrator signature (if needed): _____

FORM 2.5

Progress Summary

Date: _____

Class: _____

Baseline rates of in-seat behavior (average interval): _____

Current rate (average interval): _____

Progress toward objective: Yes   No

Maintain current plan: Yes   No

Revise current plan: Yes   No

Break Cards

BRIEF DESCRIPTION

In this behavioral plan, children earn points for either being on-task (e.g., through the beeper system) or accurately completing assignments (e.g., through the beat-the-clock game), or both. The earned points are traded in for a break card which entitles the owner to a 5-minute break from a future class activity. The teacher designates the number of points needed to acquire a break card and might require the child to earn three break cards before exchanging them for break time. The child can exchange the break cards any time she wants a "rest" from the classroom activity. For example, if the child saves 50 minutes in break cards (see Form 3.1), she can get an entire period off (unless the teacher is presenting something new or a test is planned; this condition would be written into the break card program).

TERMS

break card   a child earns points on a break card, for being on-task or completing assignments, which entitles her to a period of time off from classwork.

APPARATUS

The apparatus needed to run the break card program is a record-keeping system for points earned (see beeper system program in Chapter 1), and a record-keeping system for keeping track of break cards (see sample below):

	Earned Break Cards								
Child	1	2	3	4	5	6	7	8	9
1. S. T.	X	X	X						
2. S. W.	X	X	X	X	X	X			
3. S. B.	X	X	X	X					

Note in the above example that each time a child earns a break card by accumulating a designated number of points (e.g., 10 points), an X is placed in the appropriate column (e.g., S. T. has earned three break cards, S. W. has earned six break cards and S. B. has earned four). When a child uses a break card, the X is erased. Additionally the teacher needs to design 5-minute break cards that can be laminated (see Form 3.2 at the end of this chapter). Design enough break cards so the class will not run out.

BASELINE MEASUREMENT

Before implementing the break card program, the teacher should have had either the beeper system or the beat-the-clock game (Chapter 5) in place for 6 to 8 days. The students earn points with these management systems. On the basis of this data, a designated number of points are delineated to earn one break card of 5 minutes. Each break card earned would cost that many points.

PROCEDURES

1. Identify target children or entire class.

2. Collect baseline data on the rate of on-task behavior (using the beeper system) or assignment completion (using beat-the-clock game).

3. On the basis of the baseline data, determine how many points will be needed to buy a 5-minute break card.

4. Design a break card record-keeping system for each child.

5. Specify how many points are needed to buy a 5-minute break card.

6. When the child earns 15 minutes of break cards, she can trade them in for a break.

HOW IT WORKS

When one considers that engaging in an instructional task is usually a less-preferred activity than a host of other activities for many students, one can see that escaping such a task can become a powerful incentive (Cipani, 1990; Cipani, 1993; Cipani, 1994; Iwata, 1987; Iwata, Vollmer, & Zarcone, 1990). The break card system teaches children that they can get out of work (for a short period of time), by performing a certain amount of "well-done" work every day, and earning points for break cards. Earning time off of classwork can be a powerful incentive for children to complete their classwork. This plan capitalizes on students' desire to finish work so they can earn time off. It is extremely well suited to tasks that require much practice for students to achieve mastery, because the underlying principle is completing work accurately. Of course providing work completion or on-task behavior is also indicated, and provides the child with verbal feedback on being successful.

ADDITIONAL CONSIDERATIONS

Conditions for Break Card Use

It is important for the teacher to designate the conditions under which break cards may not be used (e.g., during a test, during presentation of new material, or during other special activities or events). The teacher should delineate in writing those situations or conditions under which the break cards may not be used. The following is a hypothetical chart delineating such situations:

Break Cards May Not Be Used Under the Following Circumstances

1. When I am giving a test.

2. When I am presenting new material to the entire class.

3. When the class has a special activity scheduled.

◆ HYPOTHETICAL EXAMPLE

Increasing On-Task Behavior in a Resource Room

Mr. Delveccio decides that the level of on-task behavior can be improved for the children who come to him in his resource room from 11 to 11:30 A.M. He uses the beeper system for a 5- to 8-day period and determines the average number of points each student earns each day. He determines how many points each child must earn to buy a 5-minute break card. Three of his students will need to earn 40 points to buy a 5-minute break card, which would result in about five break cards being purchased by the students per week (given baseline data). Four other students must earn 50 points to buy a 5-minute break card (again resulting in about four break cards earned, given baseline data).

He implements the beeper system and the children earn points. At the end of the session, the points are tallied and the children buy their break cards. These are then recorded in the record-keeping system under each child's name. Once a child has reached at least 15 minutes in break cards, she can trade them in for a break. The children who earn a break can spend that time playing board games or computer games in the resource room.

Mr. Delveccio is extremely pleased with the break card system. He has noted that the children have doubled their on-task rate in 3 weeks.

FORMS

3.1   Charting System for Tracking Each Child's Number of Earned Break Cards

Teacher records each break card earned (up to 10) for each child in the program.

3.2   Break Card

To be given to children each time they buy break cards with points; also specify when break cards may not be used.

3.3   Break Card Program: Teacher Designated Plan

Would use either form for beeper system plan or beat-the-clock game.

3.4   Progress Summary

FORM 3.1

Charting System for Tracking
Each Child's Earned Break Cards

Each time a child earns a break card with points, put a check in next column.

Earned Break Cards

	1	2	3	4	5	6	7	8	9	10	11	12
Child												
1.												
2.												
3.												
4.												
5.												
6.												
7.												
8.												
9.												
10.												
11.												
12.												
13.												
14.												
15.												
16.												
17.												
18.												
19.												
20.												

— FORM 3.2 —

Break Card

This break card entitles _____ (child's name) to _____ minutes of break. A minimum of _____ break cards must be saved before student can cash them in for time off. Break cards may not be used for the following activities:

_____

_____

_____

_____

_____

_____

```
┌──────────────── FORM 3.3 ────────────────┐

              **Break Card Program: Teacher Designated Plan**


   Child: _____


   Target behavior(s): _____On-task and/or assignment completion_____


   Designated class period(s): _____


   Baseline data across five times/sessions (designate number of points earned
   across students):


                 Days:        1. _____


                              2. _____


                              3. _____


                              4. _____


                              5. _____


   Initial number of points needed to buy 5-minute break card:_____


   Criteria for adjusting points needed up: _____


   Criteria for adjusting points needed down: _____


   Exclusion conditions:_____


   Parental consent (if needed): _____


   Administrator signature (if needed): _____

└──────────────────────────────────────────┘
```

FORM 3.4

Progress Summary

Date: _____

Class: _____

Baseline rates (points earned): _____

Current rate (points earned): _____

Progress toward objective: Yes   No

Maintain current plan: Yes   No

Revise current plan: Yes   No

Response Cards

BRIEF DESCRIPTION

Research has demonstrated that student engagement is a major factor in achievement and acquisition of material (Bickel & Bickel, 1986; Brophy & Good, 1986; Kerr & Nelson, 1993; McLaughlin, 1984). In many classrooms, teachers present curriculum content without determining whether the students understand the material. The teacher may present material for a 20-minute period, for example, without assessing each student's understanding of the content. One must realize that calling on one child to answer a question does not allow the teacher to accurately monitor how the other students in the class would respond.

The "response card" technique allows the teacher to present oral instruction or seat work assignments for short periods of time, and then check students' knowledge of the content (Narayan, Heward, Gardner, Courson, & Omness, 1990). This technique can be likened to periodic "teach-test-teach-test" instructional models. The teacher presents a certain amount of material, then poses a series of questions to all the students in the class. The students respond to the teacher's questions by writing 2- to 3-word answers on their dry-erase boards and presenting their answers to the teacher upon a signal to show their work. The teacher then surveys all the students' answers, picking up which students may be unclear about the material or readings. In contrast to selecting one student at a time to answer, the teacher can determine if most of the students have acquired the skills being taught.

For example, with a reading assignment, the teacher may designate the pages the students are to read within a certain amount of time. When they are done, the teacher poses questions about the content and the students are given a few seconds to respond using their dry-erase boards. The teacher then signals the class to show their answers. All students show their answers and the teacher scans the class, checking each student's answer.

The response card system requires a fair amount of extra work on the part of the teacher or a curriculum specialist. The teacher identifies the broad content area to be presented and then divides this set of material into small "teachable" chunks. The teacher then generates a number of questions for each chunk that measure whether students learned what the teacher intended them to learn from that material.

TERMS

None.

APPARATUS

Each student in the class must have a dry-erase board with a dry-erase pen. These can be obtained by buying a large sheet of dry-erase board at a hardware store and having the store cut the sheet into 30 or 40 smaller boards.

The teacher also needs to generate test items or questions for each chunk of the instructional material. The teacher might also "wing it" and present items once he has presented the small pieces of the topic or content area.

PROCEDURES

1. Identify content or class period in which response card system will be used and the chunks of material to be presented.

2. Give each student a dry-erase board and dry-erase pen.

3. Explain the response card system to the students.

4. Present the chunk of material or the assignment.

5. Ask a question after the presentation of material or completion of the assignment.

6. Give the students a few seconds to write their answers on their dry-erase boards, then signal them to show their answers.

7. Scan the class, praising students (a few) who gave the correct answer and present the correct answer to the class.

8. If many students made errors, present the item again.

9. Ask additional questions until the presentation has been adequately assessed.

HOW IT WORKS

This method is effective in engaging students in the instructional content, via written or oral presentation. It can be used in a variety of areas such as math, oral reading, language arts, science, spelling, and social studies. Because of the need for the students to write their responses, it may not be appropriate for kindergarten and some first-grade students (except math problems). It is an effective instructional tool as well as a system to increase students' attention to orally presented instruction or reading assignments done in class.

ADDITIONAL CONSIDERATIONS

Designing Test Items for "Chunks"

If the same textbooks are used for certain content areas across a number of classroom grades, it might be useful for a school district to assemble a team of curriculum planners who would design the test items for specific instructional chunks. These test items could be made available to all teachers teaching in that area. For example, a set of test items for each chunk could be developed for the adapted seventh-grade social studies book.

EXAMPLE OF RESPONSE CARD SYSTEM

This excerpt demonstrates teacher-presented content followed by instructional questions in which the students respond on the dry-erase board:

(Teacher presentation) Today let's discuss how to add like fractions. As you can see on the board, I have the problem $\frac{1}{3} + \frac{1}{3}$. These are like fractions in that the bottom number is the same in both fractions—that is, 3. When the bottom number is the same, in adding fractions you merely add the top numbers. In this case, $1 + 1$. You get the answer $\frac{1}{3} + \frac{1}{3} = \frac{2}{3}$.

Test question: What is $\frac{1}{4} + \frac{1}{4}$? *Begin!* (students write down answer). Ready, show (students show answer, with teacher scanning class to check everyone's answer). Okay, good. Let's try this one. What is $\frac{1}{3} + \frac{2}{3}$? *Begin!* (students write down answer). Ready, show (students show answer). Test question: Write a like fraction. *Begin!* (students write down answer). Ready, show (students show answers indicating bottom numbers of fractions are the same).

Beat the Clock

BRIEF DESCRIPTION

One method of reducing off-task behavior is to design a system that rewards children for being on-task, such as the beeper system described in Chapter 1. However, an equally effective system involves rewarding completion of the assignment for each child within a given time limit. If the child finishes an assignment in a reasonable period of time, we would expect she was on-task most of the time.

The beat-the-clock program stipulates time limits for certain class assignments, and provides reinforcement for students who finish the assignment by "beating the clock." The teacher designates on the front end which tasks are beat-the-clock tasks. For example, the teacher establishes a time limit for math, spelling, writing, and similar class assignments that require students to repeatedly practice material to facilitate long-term acquisition. New material would not be appropriate for this program. The teacher monitors the designated time limit with an oven timer.

Students who accurately complete the task within the time limit receive points (and possibly some time off at that point). Students who finish slightly after the time limit, (e.g., 3 minutes late) might receive 80% of the points to be given (i.e., a grace period). The students accrue points for a special reinforcer (this could involve break cards). To use this program, the teacher needs a quick system for checking student accuracy on the assignment, so that carelessness does not set in as the child attempts to beat the clock.

TERMS

None.

APPARATUS

Teachers need an oven timer and a task assignment chart for keeping track of the points (see Figure 5.1).

BASELINE MEASUREMENT

During a 6- to 10-day period, the teacher notes how long it takes the students to finish the target assignments by having them turn in their work (see Forms 5.1 and 5.2). The data sheet in Figure 5.2 illustrates when each student turned in a target math assignment for 3 days (by noting start time). As each student turns in an assignment (teacher checks for completion and accuracy), the teacher puts a tally mark in the appropriate column. Each column marks a 5-minute increment from start time. For example, in Figure 5.2, on 3/23, one student turned in the assignment within 15 minutes of the assignment, while 17 students completed it within 25 minutes (15 in that column plus the 2 who finished earlier).

Beat-the-Clock Task/Assignment Chart

Student(s) or class:

Task assignment:

Accuracy required:

Start time:

End time:

Grace period:

Number of points earned if finished:

Number of points earned if finished within _____ minutes (grace period):

FIGURE 5.1
A Sample Task/Assignment Chart

Assignment: Math practice-computation
Start time: 9:15 A.M.

Date/Minute	Number of Students Turning In Assignment							
	0–10	11–15	16–20	21–25	26–30	31–35	36–40	41–45
1. 3/23	0	1	1	15	12	0	3	0
2. 3/24	0	0	1	12	14	3	1	1
3. 3/25	0	0	3	14	10	2	2	1
4.	—	—	—	—	—	—	—	—
5.	—	—	—	—	—	—	—	—

FIGURE 5.2
Baseline Measurement: Tally of Students Completing Assignment

Based on this data the teacher might select 31 to 35 minutes as the initial beat-the-clock time for this math assignment.

PROCEDURES

1. Obtain baseline data for class assignments involving student practice of material (e.g., math drill and practice, spelling lists, and reading assignments). Try to *equate the amount of work* given across class assignments for the week.

2. On the basis of the baseline data, set a time limit for specific assignment.

3. Identify the number of points a student will receive upon completing the assignment accurately within the time limit (i.e., beat the clock).

4. Designate an additional grace period in which the student will receive 80% of the total points for completing assignment accurately.

5. Implement the system by informing the students that the task is a beat-the-clock task and identify the time allotted to complete the task.

6. Have a quick system for checking accuracy, including using a scoring key or scoring sheets or sampling a few student answers or items when students turn in their completed assignments.

7. If the assignment is turned in before the oven timer goes off and is accurate, assign points to the student immediately and praise her effort in completing the assignment. If there is a grace period, reset the oven timer for that time period and provide points where relevant.

8. As the students demonstrate skill at reliably achieving a time limit on a certain task, consider gradually reducing the time limit for that task until it is at a desirable reasonable level.

HOW IT WORKS

The beat-the-clock program can produce high levels of performance and on-task behavior by giving the students a goal of completing an assignment accurately and in a certain time frame. Too often, students may be given more time than they need to complete an assignment, hence they may not engage in work readily (believing they have plenty of time). By specifying a time limit, and providing points for accurate assignment completion, students will be more motivated to complete the assignment accurately without wasting time. Additionally, the game format makes it fun for children. It is also more plausible than some of the plans mentioned earlier in this section in that it does not require the teacher to constantly monitor whether the students are attending to the assignment (as is the case with the beeper system).

ADDITIONAL CONSIDERATIONS

Tasks Appropriate for Beat the Clock

It is important for the teacher to discern which tasks are appropriate for the beat-the-clock game, and which are not. To present a new academic task to the students and specify a time limit may be unreasonable, and therefore not produce desired results on student work. Before using the game, the teacher should be fairly certain that the students are capable of performing the assignment, but just need some motivation to perform it in a timely manner. Assignments that involve repetitive practice of a skill or behavior to get children to become more fluent in the skill are well suited to the beat-the-clock game.

◆ HYPOTHETICAL EXAMPLE

Use of Beat-the-Clock Game for Spelling Practice

Ms. Rodriguez decides to implement the beat-the-clock game for her class's daily spelling practice. Each day, the students are required to work on 10 spelling words for that week. During these brief sessions, the students write each spelling word 5 times, and use it in 2 sentences. By the end of the week each word will have been spelled 25 times and used in 10 sentences.

During the baseline, she specifies a 20-minute time period in which to finish the assignment. She requires the students to turn in their work whether or not they are finished at the end of the 20 minutes. Based on 6 days' worth of data, 60% of the students finish within the 20-minute period of time. She estimates that another 20% would have finished with another 5 minutes.

Based on that data, Ms. Rodriguez decides to implement the beat-the-clock game. She posts the rules of the game (see Form 5.4). She fills out a task/assignment chart each day a spelling list is assigned. She also has a master chart listing every student's name and the date with one game, because she will only use it for the spelling task. She sets the beat-the-clock time limit at 20 minutes. Students who accurately finish the assignment within 20 minutes earn 20 points each day. She gives the rest of the students a 5-minute grace period in which they can earn 15 points if they finish. Any student not finishing the assignment accurately within that time frame will not receive any points.

In the first few weeks, between 90% and 100% of the students are finishing within 20 minutes, an increase of more than 30%. Of the remaining students, all finish within the 5-minute grace period. Given this information, Ms. Rodriguez thinks she may be able to decrease the time limit for the spelling task to 16 minutes. She believes her class has definitely become more productive during this time, and there is a lot less disruptive behavior and off-task behavior.

FORMS

5.1   Baseline Measurement: Tally of Students Completing Assignment

Teacher records when each student completes a beat-the-clock assignment for baseline, indicating which time period each student finished.

5.2   Summary Baseline Measurement: Percentage of Students Completing Assignment on Time

Teacher can compute percentage of students finishing beat-the-clock task for each date it is given; allows for easy analysis of data.

5.3   Student Record System: Number of Points Earned/Beat-the-Clock Game

Teacher tracks which students earn points for each beat-the-clock game.

Notes

FORM 5.1

Baseline Measurement:
Tally of Students Completing Assignment

Assignment: _____

Start time: _____

Number of Students Turning In Assignment

Date	0–10	11–15	16–20	21–25	26–30	31–35	36–40	41–45
1. ____	____	____	____	____	____	____	____	____
2. ____	____	____	____	____	____	____	____	____
3. ____	____	____	____	____	____	____	____	____
4. ____	____	____	____	____	____	____	____	____
5. ____	____	____	____	____	____	____	____	____

FORM 5.2

Summary Baseline Measurement:
Percentage of Students Completing Assignment on Time

Assignment: _____

Time allotted: _____

Start time: _____

Percentage of Students Turning In Assignment On Time

Date of Assignment	% On Time	% During Grace	% Not On Time
1. _____	_____	_____	_____
2. _____	_____	_____	_____
3. _____	_____	_____	_____
4. _____	_____	_____	_____
5. _____	_____	_____	_____

FORM 5.3

Student Record System:
Number of Points Earned/Beat-the-Clock Game

Date:_____

Game Student	1	2	3	4	5	6	7	8	Total Points Earned
1.									
2.									
3.									
4.									
5.									
6.									
7.									
8.									
9.									
10.									
11.									
12.									
13.									
14.									
15.									

FORM 5.4

Beat the Clock:
Written Description for Class

Beat the Clock

For the following assignment(s): _____ , the class will be given a time period in which to finish this assignment completely and accurately. When an assignment is a beat-the-clock assignment, the time allowed for that assignment will be written on the board (start time and end time), and the oven timer set. You should turn in your paper once you have completed the assignment and checked it over for accuracy.

If you finish before the oven timer rings, you will receive _____ points for _____ assignments. When the oven timer rings, I will reset it for an additional 5 minutes, indicating the grace period. If you finish before the grace period is up, you earn _____ points.

Remember, stay on-task and finish your assignment. Try and you can do it.

FORM 5.5

Beat the Clock: Teacher Designated Plan

Beat-the-Clock Assignment: _____

Target class: _____

Baseline data across 5 times/sessions (designate percentage of children finished within designated time period):

Assignment: _____   1. _____

2. _____

3. _____

4. _____

5. _____

Assignment: _____   1. _____

2. _____

3. _____

4. _____

5. _____

Initial behavior standard: _____

Criteria for adjusting standard up: _____

Criteria for adjusting standard down: _____

Reinforcement for beating the clock (pts): _____

Grace period: _____

Points for finishing within grace period: _____

Parental consent (if needed): _____

Administrator signature (if needed): _____

FORM 5.6

Progress Summary

Date: _____

Assignment: _____

Class: _____

Baseline rates (percentage of children finished on time): _____

Current rate: _____

Progress toward objective: Yes   No

Maintain current plan: Yes   No

Revise current plan: Yes   No

PART 2

Plans for Reducing or Eliminating Disruptive and Rule-Violation Behavior

INTRODUCTION

What Is Disruptive Behavior?

Disruptive behavior can take many forms. Minor forms involve the following types of behavior: out-of-seat, unauthorized talking, loud talking, or other behaviors that disrupt the learning environment. In more severe forms, the disruption to the learning environment is substantial and may jeopardize the welfare and safety of the individual child, teacher, or other children. Examples of severe types of disruptive behavior include physical aggression (i.e., hitting or striking another child with an object), property destruction (i.e., grabbing and throwing a book, tearing up paper or books, or hitting the desk or wall with an abrupt and forceful action), and verbally abusive behavior (i.e., profanity, name-calling, scolding, throwing tantrums).

Classroom rule violations are also categorized as disruptive behaviors. Teachers designate rules that help them provide instruction to students in an organized and effective manner. When rules are not adhered to, the teacher's ability to present effective instruction is proportionally diminished.

The types of rule violations can range from mild to severe. Mild violations include getting out of seat without permission, talking to a peer unauthorized, chewing gum, and speaking without raising one's hand. Severe violations are the same types of behaviors described earlier under severe disruptive behaviors.

The ramifications of continued disruptive behavior are considerable. Even mild disruptive behaviors or rule violations can affect the learning environment. For example, children who are frequently out of their seats will not be able to complete many seat assignments or attend to teacher instructions. As one might imagine, eventually the children's performance deteriorates if they cannot stay in their seats long enough to learn new material.

Children who continually break class rules disrupt the classroom learning environment. For example, a child who incessantly chatters to another student during seat work not only disrupts the learning environment for him and the student he talks to, but also disrupts other students in the vicinity. Also, the teacher's ability to control the classroom environment is lessened.

Dealing with Disruptive Behavior

Teachers and other school personnel attempt to deal with disruptive behaviors and rule violations with several common strategies. I call one such strategy *rule reminder*. The teacher restates the rule when a child commits a rule violation. For example a child may get out of his seat unauthorized and the teacher may comment, "Johnny, the class rule is that you stay in your seat unless you raise your hand and ask permission to leave your seat." The child may then sit in his seat for a period of time after that reminder. However, eventually he gets out again and the teacher reminds him of the rule. The child returns to his seat. After several more unauthorized excursions out-of-seat, the teacher abandons this strategy, claiming it is useless for this child.

When restating the rule does not produce student adherence to the rules, teachers often add verbal admonishment or threats as a consequence: "Johnny you are constantly breaking the rules and getting out of your seat. Please discontinue this or I will be forced to deal with you in a more punitive manner." Once again, when this strategy does not change the child's behavior, it is discontinued, or used only intermittently.

Sometimes, teachers will establish incentives as a strategy to deal with disruptive behavior. While incentives can produce changes in a child's behavior, there are many reasons that they might not work. For example, a teacher may arrange an incentive for a child that can be earned after too long a period of time to be effective (e.g., two weeks, three weeks, a month). Some children may need something more immediate. An incentive also probably will not work if the behavior standard set by the teacher is way above the child's ability. The initial behavior standard usually does not take into account the child's current baseline level. Subsequently the child is unable to earn the incentive during the first few opportunities. Eventually the child becomes unmotivated to respond to the "possibility" of earning an incentive (not a strong possibility for him).

Finally, for more severe types of disruptive behavior, strategies such as sending the child to the principal's office or suspension or expulsion are used. A child who is repeatedly sent to the principal's office eventually does not find this consequence particularly aversive. It therefore does not deter him from engaging in further disruptive behavior. The same can be said for the suspension/expulsion strategy, which is used when the teacher and principal have tried everything they can think of and nothing has worked.

Effective Strategies for Disruptive Behavior

Teachers dealing with disruptive behavior should initially focus on increasing appropriate behavior. This effort to increase appropriate behavior should be through the use of a management strategy to increase (reinforce) on-task behaviors and completion of assignments. Disruptive behavior often can be reduced a significant degree by increasing the child's completion rate of assigned work and on-task behavior (Barrish, Saunders, & Wolf, 1969; Dietz & Repp, 1973; Speltz, Wenters-Shimamaura, & McReynolds, 1982). If on-task and attending behaviors are increased through reinforcement, the child will engage in problem behaviors less often.

The behavioral plans presented in this section frequently incorporate a classroom management strategy for on-task behaviors or assignment completion (see strategies presented in Part 1). The beeper system is usually advocated as a requisite strategy for this purpose. A specific plan for disruptive behavior then is designed to complement this overall classroom management plan for on-task behavior.

The behavioral plans discussed in detail in this section are listed in the following chart. The list also indicates whether the plans can be used as a classwide system, or for individual students, or both.

Behavioral Technique	Classwide	Individual
Good-Behavior Game	X	
Behavioral Contracting		X
Individual Disruptive Incident Barometer		X
Signal Time Out	X	X
Removal Time Out		X
Relaxation Training	X	X

The Good-Behavior Game

BRIEF DESCRIPTION

The good-behavior game is a useful strategy for a group of students or for the whole class (Barrish, Saunders, & Wolf, 1969; Harris & Sherman, 1973; Medland & Stachnik, 1972). In using this game, the teacher designates each student in the class as a member of one of several teams. The teams are posted on a bulletin board or chalkboard in the class. An acceptable level of disruptive behavior or rule violation incidents is set for the teams (called the *behavior standard*). Each team competes against the behavior standard. The students try to not engage in disruptive behaviors (however defined) or specified rule violations. Each time a student engages in a disruptive incident or rule violation, the student's team is docked a point (see Forms 6.1 and 6.2). At the end of the period, teams whose point level is at or better than the behavior standard become eligible for a lottery to pick the winner of a big prize (extra free time, special activities, and so on, depending on how often the good-behavior game is played). Teams that do not meet the standard are not eligible for the lottery for that period. The lottery drawing takes place subsequent to the period(s) in which the good-behavior game is implemented, and one team (or possibly several) is picked as the winner of the big prize. In this manner, teams that are frequently eligible for the lottery have a chance (over time) to win the big prize.

TERMS

behavior standard   the level of disruptive behavior that is considered acceptable. Teams whose frequency of disruptive behavior is above the behavior standard are not eligible for the lottery for that period.

lottery   teams become eligible for the lottery by reaching the behavior standard; one team in the lottery is selected to win a prize that period.

APPARATUS

One chart (team composition chart) lists the teams in the class and its members. Figure 6.1 illustrates a format with three teams, nine students in each team.

Once the teams are designated, a second chart (behavior monitoring chart) is used by the teacher to record instances of disruptive behavior for each team. This chart provides a quick and easy method for monitoring disruptive behavior (see Figure 6.2).

Note in Figure 6.2 that the behavior standard is designated by the solid line between 7 and 8 (indicating a standard of seven occurrences or fewer), the target disruptive behaviors delineated (i.e., out-of-seat and unauthorized talking) as well as the period the game will be used (i.e., 9:15 to 10:30 A.M.). Each time a student exhibits either out-of-seat behavior or unauthorized talking during this period, the team she is on loses a point, and the chart will be marked down one notch. At the end of the designated period, the teacher compares the rate of the target disruptive behaviors for each team with the behavior standard (i.e., 7). Teams having seven or fewer occurrences receive a star on the chart and are placed in the lottery drawing.

Team Composition Chart

Team names	Cougars	Lions	Dolphins
Students	1._____	_____	_____
	2._____	_____	_____
	3._____	_____	_____
	4._____	_____	_____
	5._____	_____	_____
	6._____	_____	_____
	7._____	_____	_____
	8._____	_____	_____
	9._____	_____	_____

FIGURE 6.1
A Sample Team Composition Chart

Behavior Monitoring Chart

Behavioral standard: 7 or fewer (see solid line)

Target behaviors: out-of-seat, unauthorized talking

Period: 9:15–10:30 A.M.

Cougars	Lions	Dolphins
1	1	1
2	2	2
3	3	3
4	4	4
5	5	5
6	6	6
7	7	7
8	8	8
9	9	9
10	10	10

FIGURE 6.2
A Sample Behavior Monitoring Chart

Depending on the needs of the class, the teacher may want to implement a second good-behavior game for a second target behavior (would require another behavior monitoring chart). In these cases, the teams must meet both standards (at or below behavior standard set for both behaviors) to be eligible for the lottery. The example in Figure 6.3 illustrates these dual criteria by presenting two charts, one for out-of-seat and another for unauthorized talking. The behavior standard for out-of-seat behavior is set at six occurrences for each team. The behavior standard for unauthorized talking is set at three for the same period. To be eligible for the lottery, a team must stay at or below six occurrences of out-of-seat incidents and at or below three for unauthorized talking.

**Behavior Monitoring Charts
for Two Target Behaviors**

Behavioral standard: <u>6 or fewer</u>

First target behavior: <u>out-of-seat</u>

Period: <u>9:15–10:30 A.M.</u>

Team A _____	Team B _____	Team C _____
1	1	1
2	2	2
3	3	3
4	4	4
5	5	5
<u>6</u>	<u>6</u>	<u>6</u>
7	7	7
8	8	8

Behavioral standard: <u>3 or fewer</u>

Second target behavior: <u>unauthorized talking</u>

Period: <u>9:15–10:30 A.M.</u>

Team A _____	Team B _____	Team C _____
1	1	1
2	2	2
<u>3</u>	<u>3</u>	<u>3</u>
4	4	4
5	5	5
6	6	6

FIGURE 6.3
Sample Behavior Monitoring Charts for Two Target Behaviors

BASELINE MEASUREMENT

Baseline data should be collected for 1 to 2 weeks. Use the behavior monitoring chart presented in either Form 6.5, 6.6, or 6.7 at the end of the chapter (forms provide for either 6, 10, or 15 occurrences of disruptive behavior). Without assigning consequences for reaching the standard, assign students to teams and just track the occurrence of target disruptive behaviors.

PROCEDURES

1. Designate a number of teams and the students that compose each team.

2. Collect baseline data on the frequency of the target behaviors for 6 to 10 days, during the designated class periods. You may or may not wish to provide students feedback on the rate of such behaviors.

3. Examine the baseline data collected. Set the behavior standard for the periods. The standard you select should reflect each team's ability to achieve that standard. It is possible that different time periods during the day might have different behavior standards.

4. Explain the good-behavior game to the students and post both the team composition chart and the behavior monitoring chart on the bulletin board.

5. Monitor and record the rate of disruptive target behavior for each team during the designated class period.

6. At the end of the class period, determine which teams achieved the behavior standard, write their names on separate pieces of paper, and place them in the lottery.

7. From the teams in the lottery, select a team that wins the big prize by randomly selecting one of the pieces of paper.

8. Across time, lower the behavior standard (i.e., less disruptive behavior) required to enter the lottery as a function of class performance.

HOW IT WORKS

The good-behavior game works by providing an achievable behavior standard for each team. Each team competes only against the standard, not against each other (as is the case in some other classroom management systems). Every team can win by reaching the standard. The standard initially sets a level of disruptive behaviors or rule violations that the teacher "can live with," realizing that as the children get better at controlling this behavior, the team level of disruptive behavior required to enter the lottery will be gradually lowered until a desirable level is achieved.

The good-behavior game also provides the teacher with the ability to provide a powerful reinforcer, one that might be too costly or not feasible for most of the class to enjoy each time. As a result of the lottery, only one team wins the big prize. But it is this chance at winning the big prize that produces all students' motivation to become eligible for the lottery. The lottery component was initially developed and tested by Dr. Brian Iwata and colleagues (Iwata, Bailey, Brown, Foshee, & Alpern, 1976). Their use of the lottery allowed them to provide an expensive prize periodically as a reinforcer to students, but not be cost prohibitive at any one time.

Selecting Team Members

The selection of team members, in most circumstances, can be up to the teacher. While some form of equating teams can be considered, remember that two components of this variation of the good-behavior game rectify any initial discrepancies among teams: (1) using baseline data to determine the standard (thereby ensuring that each team has demonstrated the capability to reach the standard and (2) use of lottery to pick the winning team from all eligible teams (thus negating the need to be on the "best" team). The teacher should try to select members for the teams that have some equity, however, the above two factors will take care of any initial judgment errors.

Provide Intermittent Praise for Nondisruptive Behavior

The teacher can intermittently scan the class and praise students who are doing their work and not engaging in disruptive behavior. Although the good-behavior game requires the teacher to monitor disruptive incidents, it should not exclude the use of praise and attention for appropriate (nondisruptive) behavior.

ADDITIONAL CONSIDERATIONS

Children Who Are More Disruptive Than Others

A potential major problem with the good-behavior game is that the behavior of the group determines the group's eligibility for the reward. It is possible that one or several children in the group might consistently alter a particular team's ability to achieve the behavior standard. This possibility is lessened by considering the baseline data in setting the initial behavior standard for the teams playing the game. However if, for example, one child on the team consistently accounts for the majority of the loss of points, the teacher may wish to consider an individual behavior contract with this child until her level of disruptive behavior approximates the lower level displayed by the other children.

Teams Compete Against a Reasonable Standard

Baseline data is very important for setting a standard. Each team competes against the behavior standard and not against each other (as was the case in the original study by Barrish, Saunders, and Wolf, 1969). By having teams compete against a standard, no team is penalized for having children who may not be capable of performing at a level that the other children in the class can perform at. The team does not have to win (i.e., display the lowest frequency of target problem behaviors) to be eligible for the lottery, but rather must only stay at or below the behavior standard. Therefore, if the standard is set at eight or fewer disruptive instances in a one-hour math class, a team that has eight occurrences is just as eligible for the lottery (that period) as a team with only two occurrences.

Providing All Teams Eligible an Additional Reinforcer

The teacher might also consider providing additional recess time, or some other inexpensive reinforcer, to all the teams achieving the standard in a given period or across a day. Therefore each team that becomes eligible for the lottery wins something, while the big prize or reinforcer is reserved for the winner of the lottery drawing.

◆ HYPOTHETICAL EXAMPLE

Use of Good-Behavior Game for a Fourth-Grade Class

Miss Roberts has considered developing a management strategy to reduce out-of-seat and unauthorized talking behavior in her class. Although there are only a few students who are extremely problematic in these areas, even small levels of such behaviors across 27 other children can create a noisy and unruly classroom.

She selects two 40-minute periods (math and language arts periods) in her fourth-grade class to implement the good-behavior game. She designates the teams and the members of each team, then collects data for 7 days on the rate of such behaviors for every member on the teams. Each time a child either gets out-of-seat or engages in unauthorized talking, it counts as an occurrence for that child's team. After examining the baseline data (which indicated a rate of behavior between 10 and 15 for all teams in math and 12 to 21 in language arts), Miss Roberts designates the following behavior standards: math 14, spelling 18. Each team must stay at or below this level of disruptive behavior to be eligible for the lottery.

She then implements the good-behavior game during the math and language arts periods. She informs the class of the rules of the good-behavior game and places the rules on the bulletin board: (1) Do not get out of your seat without permission and (2) do not talk to other students. Dry erase board will be used to record the occurrence of target behaviors for each team on the behavior monitoring chart. Miss Roberts decides that each team that becomes eligible for the lottery will earn 4 extra minutes of free time at the end of the day. Additionally, one winning team (drawn from the eligible teams in the lottery) for each period will get to choose a reinforcer from a "grab bag," consisting of eight or nine special reinforcers (e.g., a 5-minute time off ticket for math or spelling, being the first team to be discharged to lunch or recess, pizza party, popcorn party). Because the pizza party is more expensive, she places only 1 ticket in the grab bag. Events that do not cost money have 10 to 12 tickets (thus increasing the probability of selecting those).

Miss Roberts implements this system and records the occurrence of disruptive behavior on the behavior monitoring chart under the team the child is a member of. At the end of the period, she determines which teams are eligible for the lottery drawing. She selects one team to enter the grab bag. One member of that team comes up and chooses the team's prize out of the grab bag.

Across the first 2 weeks of the good-behavior game, the rate of disruptive behavior has dropped below 10 on every day for each team during math and language arts periods. On the basis of this data, Miss Roberts now selects a new behavior standard—8—as the goal needed for a team to be eligible for the lottery. She realizes that eventually the class will reach her terminal goal of four or fewer occurrences of disruptive behavior during math and language arts.

◆ HYPOTHETICAL EXAMPLE

Increasing Appropriate Behavior in a Seventh-Grade Science Class

Mr. Jones teaches a seventh-grade science class. Although the students are fairly well behaved, he would like to increase the rate of answers to oral questions during his lecture. Mr. Jones uses a teaching style in which he presents information and then asks students questions on the information. Until now the rate of answers to his questions has been fairly low. He would like for the students to become more engaged in his lecture by answering these questions in a more earnest fashion. He decides to use the good-behavior game for three of his six class periods to test its efficacy.

During these three periods, he designates three to five teams (depending on number of students). He collects 8 days of baseline data on the rate of question-answering behavior for each team. Based on the baseline data (which indicated a rate of between one and four questions answered in a 50-minute period), he designated the behavior standard as three or more questions answered accurately, by a team. Achieving the standard would make the team eligible for the lottery.

On the behavior monitoring chart, the occurrence of appropriate question-answering behavior during each period will be recorded on the dry erase board for each team. He decides that each team that becomes eligible for the lottery will win 2 extra minutes of time to get to class at the beginning of the following period, without being marked tardy. The winner of the lottery will randomly select one of eight or nine special reinforcers, which will include prizes such as homework passes, extra bonus points on tests, and a video party hour.

After informing the class of the rules of the good-behavior game, Mr. Jones implements the system and records the occurrence of question-answering behavior for each team (based on which student answered the question correctly). In the first 2 weeks of the good-behavior game, the rate of question-answering behavior increases to 10 or more for each period. Correct answers to questions increase to more than 70% of the total questions asked. The good-behavior game has helped Mr. Jones reach his goal for the class on question answering. He will maintain its use throughout the year to monitor students' attention to his lectures.

FORMS

Notes

FORM 6.1

Written or Oral Description of Good-Behavior Game for Class

Older Children

The good-behavior game involves teams of students trying to behave appropriately to become eligible for the lottery. Each team tries to stay at or below the behavior standard, which is the number above the solid line on the chart.

Each team has the opportunity to be eligible for the lottery drawing. Teams in the lottery become eligible to win one of several prizes. One team is selected from those who are in the lottery, after the following time period _____ .

The good-behavior game will be played in the following period(s) _____ .

The rules of the good-behavior game are to *not:* _____ .

Each time a child engages in one of these behaviors, the child's team will be marked down a number. Each team must remain at or below the following number _____ .

FORM 6.2

Written or Oral Description of Good Behavior Game for Class

Younger Children

We are going to play the good-behavior game. To play, everyone will be on a team. When we play the good-behavior game during _____ (specify periods or times), I will let everyone know we are playing the game. I will post this chart with each team on the bulletin board. Each time someone on a team does any of the following behaviors _____ that person's team will be marked down a number. If your team is below the mark by the number _____ at the end of the period, your team's name goes on a slip of paper and is placed into the fishbowl. I will pick one team out of the fishbowl to win a prize. We will then play the good-behavior game again so that another team might win. Try your best.

FORM 6.3

Good-Behavior Game: Teacher Designated Plan

Designated team(s): _____

Disruptive or rule violation behavior(s):   (1) _____

                                              (2) _____

                                              (3) _____

Designated class period(s) for good-behavior game: _____

Baseline data (sessions or days): _____

Team _____ (1) _____   Team _____ (1)_____

              (2)_____   (2)_____

              (3)_____   (3)_____

              (4)_____   (4)_____

              (5)_____   (5)_____

              Mean frequency _____   Mean frequency _____

Initial behavioral standard: _____

Criteria for adjusting standard up: _____

Criteria for adjusting standard down: _____

Reinforcement for all teams reaching lottery: _____

Major prize for lottery winner: _____

Parental consent (if needed): _____

Administrator signature (if needed):_____

FORM 6.4

Progress Summary

Date: _____

Class: _____

Average baseline rates of target disruptive behavior (across all teams): _____

Current rate (across all teams): _____

Progress toward objective: Yes   No

Maintain current plan: Yes   No

Revise current plan: Yes   No

FORM 6.5

Behavior Monitoring Chart

Class: _____

Behavior(s): _____

Behavior standard: _____

Time period(s): _____

Team _____   Team _____   Team _____   Team _____   Team _____

1	1	1	1	1
2	2	2	2	2
3	3	3	3	3
4	4	4	4	4
5	5	5	5	5
6	6	6	6	6

FORM 6.6

Behavior Monitoring Chart

Class: _____

List target disruptive behavior(s): _____

Behavior standard: _____

Time period(s): _____

Team _____	Team _____	Team _____	Team _____	Team _____
1	1	1	1	1
2	2	2	2	2
3	3	3	3	3
4	4	4	4	4
5	5	5	5	5
6	6	6	6	6
7	7	7	7	7
8	8	8	8	8
9	9	9	9	9
10	10	10	10	10

FORM 6.7

Behavior Monitoring Chart

Class: _____

List target disruptive behavior(s): _____

Behavior standard: _____

Time period(s): _____

Team _____	Team _____	Team _____	Team _____	Team _____
1	1	1	1	1
2	2	2	2	2
3	3	3	3	3
4	4	4	4	4
5	5	5	5	5
6	6	6	6	6
7	7	7	7	7
8	8	8	8	8
9	9	9	9	9
10	10	10	10	10
11	11	11	11	11
12	12	12	12	12
13	13	13	13	13
14	14	14	14	14
15	15	15	15	15

Behavioral Contracting

BRIEF DESCRIPTION

In some cases, the disruptive behavior of only a few students is of concern to the teacher. The teacher may feel comfortable with his general classroom management strategy for the class as a whole, but may need specific strategies for a few individual students. Behavioral contracting is well suited for these circumstances (Homme, 1970; Homme, Csanyi, Gonzales, & Rechs, 1970). A behavioral contract is a simple arrangement that links an individual child's behavior with long-term rewards or incentives. Behavior contracts usually cover a long period of time (e.g., 2, 3, or 4 weeks). The length of time is called the *contract period*.

The child's behavior is evaluated daily against a certain behavior standard (called a *daily behavior standard*). The contract specifies the number of days the child must achieve the behavior standard (called *contract terms*). If the child satisfies the contract terms, a reinforcer specified in the contract is provided. The contract also specifies when, where, and how much of the reinforcer is delivered to the child. Once one contract has been met, the teacher can write a new behavioral contract to cover another period of time. Therefore, over the course of a term or semester, several successive contracts may be written. For example, the teacher may write one behavioral contract for the first 2 weeks, another behavioral contract for the next 3 weeks, a third one for the following 3 weeks, and so on.

TERMS

daily behavior standard   the level of disruptive behavior that is considered acceptable for a given day.

contract period   the length of time the contract is in force.

contract terms   the behavioral obligations of the child and the reinforcers that are earned if the contract terms are met. How many times (or percentage of total) the child must achieve daily behavior standard over the contract period.

APPARATUS

A hypothetical sample behavioral contract is presented in Figure 7.1 (see Form 7.1 or 7.5 for blank forms). The contract illustrates the basic components of the behavioral contracting method. Within the contract, the teacher identifies the behavior standard for each day (i.e., two or fewer occurrences of verbal abuse). The teacher also identifies the number of days in the contract period that the child will have to meet the behavior standard (6 of 10 days). Finally, contingent upon the child meeting the contract terms, the reinforcers that will be delivered, as well as when and how they will be delivered are specified (e.g., allowed to play with Game Boy during recess). The child (if applicable) would have a copy of the contract along with teacher.

Behavioral Contract

Target child: R. F.

Class: Ms. Ryback's Fourth Grade

Target child behavior: Verbal abuse—any occurrence of yelling, screaming above a conversation tone, or profanity directed toward other students while on playground.

Behavior standard: Two or fewer occurrences in a day (incorporates several playground periods).

Length of contract: 2 weeks

Contract terms: Must achieve behavior standard 6 of 10 days (not including absences) during contract period. Absences extend time period until 10 school days have been accrued.

Teacher obligations: If R. F. meets contract terms, Ms. Ryback will allow R. F. to bring to school his Game-Boy within 4 days of meeting contract terms to play with during one of the recesses that day.

Criteria for new contract:

1. Meeting current contract terms—new contract will be drawn up the following day.

2. Failing to meet contract terms—a minimum of a 4-day wait period before new contract is drawn up.

FIGURE 7.1
A Sample Behavioral Contract

BASELINE MEASUREMENT

Baseline data on the frequency of the target disruptive behavior should be collected for at least a contract term. Form 7.4 at the end of this chapter can be used.

PROCEDURES

1. Identify target children.

2. Identify target behavior, either undesirable behavior (to decrease) such as disruptive behavior, or desirable behavior (to increase) such as the number of times hand is raised appropriately.

3. Collect baseline data on frequency of behavior for each target child.

4. Based on the baseline data, set the behavior standard (i.e., frequency of behavior deemed acceptable for each day) and designate how behavior will be monitored.

5. With the child, set the contract terms of the behavioral contract indicating how many days the behavior standard must be achieved within the contract period.

6. Designate what reinforcers the child would like to earn as a function of meeting the contract terms.

7. Implement the behavior monitoring system (see Form 7.4).

8. If the child reaches the behavior standard for the day, check it on the contract chart. If the child meets the contract terms at the end of the contract period, deliver the reinforcer at the designated time and place.

9. If the child does not meet the obligations of the contract, end the current contract and consider writing a new one after a break of one to several days (so as not to teach the child to break contracts indiscriminately).

HOW IT WORKS

The utility of the behavioral contract is in its ability to target children who are having more difficulty than the rest of the class. The behavior standard must be determined through baseline data and set so that the child will achieve success with the first several contracts. The teacher may need to be content initially with a higher behavior standard than the ultimate target goal in the beginning of the program.

As the child achieves success and experiences the reward, she will be more motivated to behave appropriately to meet the contracts that are subsequently set up. The teacher then shapes the child's level of disruptive behavior to lower numbers of occurrences by gradually moving the behavior standard closer to the desired goal. For example, after a child meets the contract terms by staying under three disruptive incidents per day for 8 of 10 days, the next behavioral contract might require no more than two disruptive incidents per day for 6 out of the next 10 days.

ADDITIONAL CONSIDERATIONS

Inaccurate Baseline Data

Occasionally, the baseline data collected might underestimate the level of disruptive behavior. Therefore the teacher might set a higher initial behavior standard than what the child is capable of performing. The teacher should suspect that this is the case if the child doesn't succeed in the first several behavioral contracts. If the child misses the first few contracts for whatever reason, reevaluate the behavior standard on the basis of the child's performance on the last several behavioral contracts. Then reestablish a new behavior standard that is more within reach of the child.

Strengthen Reinforcers

If a child fails the first few behavioral contracts, another reason may be that the reinforcer being used is not "potent" enough. In most cases, when children are involved in deciding the reinforcer they are to earn, potency is usually not the issue. However if the child is either not interested in that reinforcer, or can get it elsewhere without having to meet a contract, then it may not be sufficiently attractive to motivate the child. In those cases, consider finding another reinforcer to use in the contract.

Application for Aggressive Behavior

For behaviors like aggression, one may set the behavior standard at 0 occurrences for a given day or even time period so that nonaggression is reinforced. However, some children may be unable to meet contract terms that require 5 days of nonaggression. In those cases, the contracts can be designed to provide an achievable standard. For example, the contract terms may require the child to achieve only a certain proportion of days or time periods with 0 occurrences to allow him to meet with success. If a child is aggressive once or twice a day, the behavior standard might be set at 0 occurrences for 2-hour blocks of time during the day (i.e., three 2-hour blocks during a school day). The contract terms might require the child to meet the standard at least 2 of 3 blocks per day, for 4 consecutive days. This would be a more reasonable standard for this child, in contrast to requiring 5 straight days of 0 occurrences of aggression. Remember, when setting the behavior standard and the contract terms, be guided by baseline data!

◆ HYPOTHETICAL EXAMPLE

Dealing with Physical Aggression

Renaldo has had a history of physical aggression toward other children. The school has previously attempted suspensions, in-school suspensions, parent conferences, and time outs. However, none of these efforts has resulted in a change in Renaldo's aggressive behavior. Mrs. Ralph decides to implement a behavioral contract for Renaldo. She sets up a behavioral contract that gives Renaldo points during time periods in which he refrains from aggressive behavior. She defines *aggression* as hitting another child. She decides to observe Renaldo for a 1-week period to collect baseline data. He engages in aggressive behavior between 0 and 2 occurrences per day.

Renaldo also pushes and shoves other children. She collects baseline data on his rate of pushing and shoving for a week. Renaldo is pushing and shoving other children between 1 and 4 times a day.

Based on this information Mrs. Ralph sets the behavior standard for a 1-hour block of time. Renaldo will earn 5 points if he does not engage in any aggressive behavior or pushing and shoving other children during that time period. Therefore the school day is divided into five 1-hour blocks. The first contract period is for 1 week. At the end of the week, if Renaldo has earned 15 or more points each day, for all 5 days, he is allowed to have 20 more minutes of extra recess Friday afternoon (along with his classmates).

Mrs. Ralph implements the plan after reviewing it with Renaldo. The program is a success! He earns extra recess for the first four behavioral contracts. Mrs. Ralph then changes the contract terms to require Renaldo to earn 20 points a day each day of the week to earn extra Friday recess. She hopes that within 3 months Renaldo will be able to refrain from hitting, pushing, or shoving other children for several weeks at a time.

◆ HYPOTHETICAL EXAMPLE

Increasing Appropriate Behavior

Sarah has started coming late to class after recess period. Each day there are four recess periods, and Sarah is late coming in from recess after at least two of the four periods. On some days she is late all four times. Mrs. Wildman has attempted to intervene by discussing this with Sarah and her parents as well as constantly reminding Sarah to come back to class on time. None of these efforts has worked.

Mrs. Wildman decides to set up a behavioral contract with Sarah to get her to come back from recess on time. With the baseline data indicating between two and four tardies, Mrs. Wildman sets the daily behavior standard of coming in from recess on time at two or more times. Each time Sarah is on time, she will receive one check, with a maximum of four earned checks per day. Sarah must achieve the daily behavior standard on 11 of 15 days to meet the contract terms. Absences are not included in this contract. *Being tardy* is defined as failing to be in the classroom after the class door is closed (signifying the end of recess). Mrs. Wildman will blow the whistle twice, signaling the time for all children to line up in front of the door to the class. A minute later, the students in line come inside the classroom.

Mrs. Wildman goes over the behavioral contract with Sarah and Sarah agrees to the terms. If Sarah meets the contract terms, she will then be given a 1-hour record and dance party with all her classmates on the next Friday in which the contract is met. If she does not meet the contract, 5 days must elapse before a new contract is written up. Additionally if Sarah does not come in on time for a given recess period, Mrs. Wildman will simply go out and get Sarah and bring her into class. She will not get a check for that period.

Sarah meets the first set of contract terms, thus earning a dance party that Friday. Mrs. Wildman continues the use of behavioral contracts to facilitate Sarah's coming in from recess on time. After four additional behavioral contracts, with three of them being successful, Mrs. Wildman sets the behavior standard at four out of four recesses being on time, for 10 out of 15 days, to meet the contract terms. The goal of being on time every day is now a possibility.

◆ HYPOTHETICAL EXAMPLE

Limited Application of Behavioral Contract for Tardiness

Down the hall, Mr. James' eighth-grade class has trouble being on time for English Composition class. Mr. James has between 25 and 30 students in this class in fourth period. Baseline data across 7 days revealed the following rates of tardiness per day among the 25 or 30 students in the class: 7, 12, 5, 9, 16, 10, 8. Mr. James designs a behavioral contract for the entire class. He defines *tardiness* as any student scheduled to be in his class that day who is not in his or her seat when the bell sounds. He does not include excused absences. He sets the contract period at 5 days. The daily classwide behavior standard is 8 or fewer tardies for that period. The contract terms require the class to achieve this behavior standard only two of five days the first week. If the class meets the contract terms, Mr. James will allow the class to choose an activity during half of the science period that Friday, provided the activity is not disruptive to other classes in the building.

The students achieve the behavior standard twice in the first 5 days, meeting the contract terms. As a result Mr. James writes a new behavioral contract requiring the class to meet the behavior standard 3 days out of 5 to earn an activity of their choice on Friday.

FORMS

7.1   Behavioral Contract: Teacher Designated Plan

7.2   Progress Summary

7.3   Sample Behavioral Contract

Posted and available to student. Teacher can fill in blanks when writing a contract for student.

7.4   Baseline Daily Frequency of Behavior Chart

Teacher can use this data sheet for two target behaviors, if needed, just circling next highest number with each occurrence.

7.5   Sample Behavioral Contract

Generic form.

— FORM 7.1 —

Behavioral Contract: Teacher Designated Plan

Target child: _____

Target behavior(s)—(define each behavior) _____

_____

Contract period: _____

Baseline data across 8 days (designate either *frequency* or *proportion*):

(1) _____   (6) _____

(2) _____   (7) _____

(3) _____   (8) _____

(4) _____   Mean frequency: _____

(5) _____   range: _____

Target behavioral goal: _____

Daily behavioral standard: _____

Contract terms: _____

Criteria for altering contract after failure: _____

Criteria for altering behavioral standard: _____

Criteria for altering contract terms: _____

Reinforcer for meeting contract terms: _____

Who will implement plan: _____

Parental consent (if needed): _____

Administrator signature: _____

_____

FORM 7.2

Progress Summary

Date: _____

Class: _____

Baseline rates (mean and range): _____

Current rate (mean and range): _____

Progress toward objective:	Yes	No
Maintain current plan:	Yes	No
Revise current plan:	Yes	No

FORM 7.3

Sample Behavioral Contract

Target child: _____

Class: _____

Target child behavior: _____

Daily behavior standard: _____

Length of contract: _____

Contract terms: _____

Teacher obligations: _____

Criteria for new contract: _____

Met daily behavioral standard?

Days   Yes / No

1.

2.

3.

4.

5.

6.

7.

8.

9.

Number of days standard met: _____

FORM 7.4

Baseline Daily Frequency of Behavior Chart

Child's name: _____

Contract period: _____

Contract terms: _____

Target behavior 1: _____

    1   2   3   4   5   6   7   8   9   10   11   12

Target behavior 2: _____

    1   2   3   4   5   6   7   8   9   10   11   12

── FORM 7.5 ──

Sample Behavioral Contract

Target child: _____

Class: _____

Target child behavior: _____

Behavior standard: _____

Length of contract: _____

Contract terms: _____

Teacher obligations: _____

Criteria for new contract: _____

_____

Individual Disruptive
Incident Barometer

BRIEF DESCRIPTION

The individual disruptive incident barometer program allows the teacher to monitor the occurrence of the child's target disruptive behaviors by plotting each occurrence on the individual child's disruptive incident barometer. Each time the child engages in a target disruptive behavior, the barometer is moved down one level (see Form 8.1). A behavior standard is identified, through baseline data, which determines the "acceptable" level of disruptive behavior. The behavior standard is then depicted as a solid line drawn between two levels on the individual disruptive incident barometer. If the child stays at or below this target level on the barometer, reinforcement occurs at the end of the period (or day, depending on the length of time it is used).

The disruptive incident barometer is a visually pleasing display that monitors the rate of disruptive behaviors of given children. The visual display (on a bulletin board or poster, or on the child's desk in an erasable medium) presents a barometer with numbered levels (for younger children, you can use letters or different colors). Each level corresponds to an act of disruptive behavior. As a child engages in a disruptive behavior, the teacher circles or marks the next level, moving the child closer to the behavior standard, or the point at which the child loses the reinforcer. A solid line drawn between two levels (e.g., between the numbers 7 and 8) indicates the behavior standard.

TERMS

behavior standard   the level of disruptive behavior that is considered acceptable. The standard identifies the target level for the barometer, the rate at or above which the child earns the reinforcer.

APPARATUS

The barometer featured in Column A illustrates a plan that provides for 10 levels (i.e., 10 occurrences of disruptive behavior for a given period). The behavior standard is at or above Level 7 (therefore child must not engage in disruptive behavior more than 4 times). The barometer featured in Column B illustrates a system with 20 levels, with the standard for reinforcement at or above Level 13. Obviously, the longer the period of time the individual disruptive incident barometer program is in effect (e.g., half an hour versus 3 hours) the more levels are needed for the barometer.

The disruptive incident barometer itself can be illustrated in several ways:

- Paper chart on the child's desk
- Individually laminated chart on each child's desk
- Individually laminated chart on teacher's desk

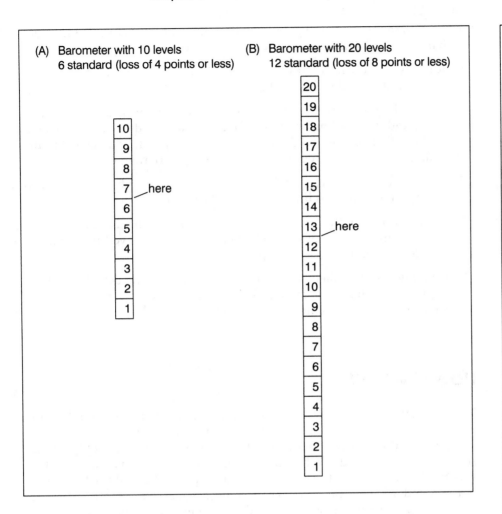

(A) Barometer with 10 levels
6 standard (loss of 4 points or less)

(B) Barometer with 20 levels
12 standard (loss of 8 points or less)

BASELINE MEASUREMENT

Use the barometer apparatus for 5 to 8 days in the target time period, to collect data on the rate of disruptive behavior for each child who will be in the program. On the basis of this data, the behavior standard can be determined. Form 8.2 at the end of the chapter can be used for this.

PROCEDURES

1. Identify target children.

2. Identify target disruptive behaviors, i.e., disruptive behavior that will result in loss of a level.

3. Collect baseline data on the rate of disruptive behaviors of the target children or entire class for 4 to 7 days (if representative of other days in terms of levels of occurrence).

4. Designate the time periods you will implement the disruptive incident barometer program (or across the entire day).

5. Identify the initial behavior standard and what reinforcer will be earned if the child meets the behavior standard.

6. Design the disruptive incident barometer with appropriate number of levels and draw a line below the behavior standard level (e.g., a solid dark line between 4 and 5 on a chart with 10 points indicates that the child earns the reinforcer if she doesn't lose more than 6 points).

7. When a target disruptive behavior occurs, move the barometer down one by coloring or circling the next highest level.

8. At end of designated period (e.g., at end of 1 hour, 2 hours, before noon, entire day), determine whether the child achieved the standard and deliver reinforcer if appropriate.

9. Continue to implement the individual disruptive incident barometer, adjusting the behavior standard to require a lower frequency of disruptive behavior to achieve behavior standard.

HOW IT WORKS

The individual disruptive behavior barometer sets a behavior standard for an acceptable level of disruptive behavior, and, when achieved, results in a powerful reinforcer being delivered. It allows the teacher to set an initial standard for an individual child that is achievable (given that baseline data was used to determine the initial standard). Once the child achieves the initial standard, the standard can become progressively more stringent, thus reducing disruptive behavior to desirable levels gradually but systematically. The barometer's use in research studies, as a technique termed *differential reinforcement of low rates of behavior*, has been extremely successful (Dietz & Repp, 1973; Zwald & Gresham, 1982).

ADDITIONAL CONSIDERATIONS

When a Child Falls Below the Barometer Line

In some cases, when a child falls below the barometer line, indicating her loss of the reinforcer for that time period, she may become more difficult until the next barometer is put into place (e.g., child loses chance to earn reinforcer at 2:30 because she went past barometer line at 11:45). This can be handled in one of several effective and acceptable ways. However, one way that is unacceptable is to change the behavior standard, or the previous recording of disruptive behavior, as a function of the child's lack of success in achieving a behavior standard on a given day. The changing of the behavior standard must be made before the beginning of the barometer program for that day or period. Don't change simply because the child failed; that sends the message that when the child fails to generate enough self-control on a given day, we will alter the standard. If this is done often, the child's behavior will be less likely to change systematically, but rather it will appear that teacher behavior changes to accommodate whatever the student does.

One requirement for handling a failure to achieve the behavior standard is the continuance of the program, with teacher "riding out" the temporary increase in disruptive behavior. The teacher may have a tough time that day, but with a new barometer program the next day or period, the child has a whole new chance to reach the standard and will certainly remember what happened the previous day when she failed to regulate her behavior (i.e., she will learn that there is a consequence for not demonstrating appropriate behavior).

This temporary "storm" can be lessened by designing shorter time periods for the barometer program. For example, if the period for the barometer program was initially set at the whole day, the teacher might consider having two barometer programs, one in the morning and a new one in the afternoon. Then the child could start fresh each half-day. Or a new barometer program could begin every 2 hours. The designation of the length of time for the barometer program is best done by consulting the data and the child's behavior.

Another method for lessening the effect of the child's disruptive behavior is to use a graded system. For example, on a 20-level barometer system, the child earns 5 extra minutes of recess time if she stays above Level 14, 3 extra minutes if she stays above Level 11, and 1 extra minute if she stays above Level 8. This provides an incentive on any given day to keep trying.

Inaccurate Baseline Data

Occasionally, the baseline data collected might underestimate the level of disruptive behavior. Therefore the teacher might set a lower initial behavior standard for the disruptive behavior barometer than the child is capable of achieving. For example, a behavior standard set at 4 might be unreasonable if the baseline data should have revealed more than 8 occurrences per day. Suspect that this is the case if the child doesn't succeed with the first several barometers. Reevaluate the behavior standard on the basis of the child's performance on the last several barometers (e.g., child stayed below 8 incidents in last three barometers). Then reestablish a new behavior standard to be more within reach of the child.

Strengthen Reinforcers

If a child fails to access the reinforcer in the first few barometers, another reason may be that the reinforcer being used is not "potent" enough. In most cases, when children are involved in deciding the reinforcer they are to earn, potency is usually not the issue. However, if the child is either not interested in that reinforcer, or can get it elsewhere without having to meet the barometer standard, then it may not be sufficiently attractive to motivate the child. In those cases, consider finding another reinforcer to use with the barometer program.

◆ HYPOTHETICAL EXAMPLE

Reducing Teasing

R. K. teases several other students in the class. It is obviously annoying to the children being teased, as well as other children in the vicinity. Mr. Baros is concerned about this behavior, both for its effect on the other children as well as on R. K. He has talked to R. K. multiple times about how his teasing is hurtful to the other children, but this does not deter him from teasing children the next day. Mr. Baros has also used time out, but without success. He notes that R. K. likes physical education class and enjoys helping the instructor. After talking with the instructor, Mr. Baros obtains his consent to use a special reinforcer for R. K. if he meets a behavioral goal.

Mr. Baros sets up a disruptive incident barometer after obtaining the following baseline frequency of R. K.'s teasing across 5 days: 9, 12, 15, 6, 10. He designs a disruptive incident barometer that goes up to 20 and sets the behavior standard between 10 and 11. Each time R. K. teases someone, he will lose a point, starting from 1. R. K. can lose up to 10 points and still achieve the standard for that day. However if R. K. teases 11 or more times that day, he does not earn the reinforcer. Mr. Baros explains the program to R. K. in which he will remove a point each time R. K. engages in teasing behavior. Mr. Baros is careful to point out what constitutes teasing behavior and suggests alternative things he might say (e.g., compliments or questions). If R. K. meets the behavior standard for all the days before the next physical education period, he will be allowed to help the instructor for 10 minutes during the next class. (Physical education class meets twice a week, Wednesday and Friday.)

FORMS

8.1   Individual Disruptive Incident Barometer Agreement

Can be posted for child's view.

8.2   Individual Incident Barometer Program: Teacher Designated Plan

8.3   Progress Summary

FORM 8.1

Individual Disruptive Incident Barometer Agreement

Rule: Whenever _____ (child's name) engages in the following

disruptive behavior(s): _____ you move one level down on

the disruptive incident barometer. You lose a level each time you engage in _____

_____ . If the barometer stays above the solid line, drawn between

_____ and _____ , you earn _____ .

Disruptive Behaviors

     1.

     2.

     3.

     4.

Remember, being considerate of the teacher and your classmates and following class rules <u>pays off!</u>

─────── FORM 8.2 ───────

Individual Incident Barometer Program:
Teacher Designated Plan

Target child: _____

Target disruptive behavior(s): _____

_____

Designated time period(s): _____

Number of levels of incident barometer: _____

Present baseline data across 5 days/sessions:

1. _____

2. _____

3. _____

4. _____

5. _____

Target behavioral standard: _____

Initial behavioral standard (number of points that can be lost before losing reinforcement): _____

Line drawn between which two numbers: _____

Criteria for adjusting standard up: _____

Criteria for adjusting standard down: _____

Reinforcer earned for reaching behavioral standard: _____

Who will implement plan: _____

Parental consent (if needed): _____

Administrator signature: _____

_____

FORM 8.3

Progress Summary

Date: _____

Child: _____

Baseline rate: _____

Current rate: _____

Progress toward objective:	Yes	No
Maintain current plan:	Yes	No
Revise current plan:	Yes	No

9

Signal Time Out for Minor
Disruptive Behavior

BRIEF DESCRIPTION

To address minor disruptive behaviors, this program combines a signal time out with a reinforcement plan for on-task behaviors (e.g., the beeper system). Unlike the removal time out described in Chapter 10, the signal time out procedure does not entail removing the children from the area or classroom (Foxx & Shapiro, 1978; Salend & Gordon, 1987; Yeager & McLaughlin, 1995). Rather, the children remain in their seats. However they cannot earn any points during the signal time out period.

The signal time out period is specified by the placement of a badge, sticker, or card on the student's desk or tag board for a designated minimum time period. In the initial empirical study, a badge was used (Foxx & Shapiro, 1978). However, if the child continues disruptive behavior during the time out, the time period can be extended until the child quiets down. If more severe disruptive behavior occurs during the signal time out period, the teacher may use the removal time out procedure, to avoid jeopardizing the safety of other students or their learning experience.

TERMS

minor disruptive behaviors   behaviors that do not cause a major disruption to the learning environment or do not present a dangerous condition to the child or others.

APPARATUS

The specific form of the signal time out needs to be designated. In some cases it can be a card placed on the student's desk or a tag board with a list of students on signal timeout at any given time. With young children, a sticker or badge can be used. In addition, an oven timer should be used to keep track of the length of time the child remains in the signal time out.

BASELINE MEASUREMENT

The disruptive behaviors that produce a signal time out need to be delineated (see Form 9.3 at the end of this chapter). Each behavior could be coded and scored as to its frequency of occurrence. Form 9.1 at the end of this chapter allows up to four behaviors to be measured over a 5-day period. A sample with hypothetical data is shown in Figure 9.1.

PROCEDURES

1. Define the target disruptive behaviors that constitute minor disruptive behavior (e.g., getting out-of-seat, talking out, talking to peers, or making unnecessary noise).

**Frequency of Disruptive
Behavior Data Sheet**

Child's name (or entire class): <u>Entire fourth-grade class</u>

Period: <u>Reading/Language Arts 10–11 A.M.</u>

Behavior/Date	6–7	6–8	6–9	6–10	6–11	Total/Week
(1) Unauthorized talking	༔ Ⅱ	Ⅲ	༔ Ⅰ	༔	༔	26
(2) Out-of-seat	Ⅲ	༔ Ⅱ	Ⅲ	༔	༔ Ⅰ	24

Figure 9.1
A Sample Data Sheet for Frequency of Disruptive Behavior

2. Implement the beeper system to reward on-task behavior and collect baseline data on the rate of minor disruptive behaviors.

3. Specify minimum signal time out period.

4. When a minor disruptive behavior occurs, the signal (e.g., a badge, sticker, or ribbon) is placed at the child's desk or tag board, or, in the case of younger children, on their person.

5. Set the timer for the minimum signal time out length.

6. The child does not receive points for being on-task during the signal time out period.

7. If minor disruptive behaviors continue during signal time out period, do not remove signal until child is quiet.

8. If more severe disruptive behavior occurs during the time out period, use the removal time out program (discussed in Chapter 10) for severe disruptive behavior.

9. When the signal time out period is over, remove the signal time out. The child can then begin earning points for being on-task.

HOW IT WORKS

Signal time outs can be effective by removing the opportunity to earn points for appropriate classroom behavior (i.e., being on-task). If the points can be traded in for powerful incentives, the child will be motivated to stay on-task and do his work. By reinforcing on-task behavior as part of the overall plan, the use of the signal time out for disruptive behavior increases the students' motivation to engage in appropriate on-task behavior and avoid getting a signal time out.

ADDITIONAL CONSIDERATIONS

Setting a Minimum Signal Time Out Length

The minimum length of the signal time out should be a period of time that would entail the student losing at least one opportunity to earn points (i.e., at least one beep). Therefore if the beeps average one every 3 minutes, the minimum length should be set for at least 3 minutes. While that doesn't ensure that at least one beep will occur in the signal time out (because some intervals between beeps may be longer than 3 minutes), it does provide a good basis for the minimum time out period.

Altering the Density of Beeps on the Beeper System

In using the signal time out procedure, if the rate of disruptive behavior does not decrease, consider increasing the number of beeps that occur during the period(s). This would make points more frequently available and provide a greater opportunity to catch the children being on-task and not engaging in disruptive behavior. Also examine the reinforcers that back up the points to determine if these might be changed or enhanced to act as more powerful incentives for on-task behavior.

◆ HYPOTHETICAL EXAMPLE

Group Application for "Chatter"

A third-grade teacher wants to decrease the frequency of chatter among students during the reading period. Part of her problem is her inability to detect all who are talking. She decides to implement a group plan for a 3-minute signal time out along with the beeper system. These minutes would ensure that at least one and possibly two to three beeps would occur during the signal time out period. Contingent upon class chatter reaching a detectable level, a yellow card will be placed on the teacher's desk for everyone to see. The oven timer will be set for 3 minutes. During this time, no student will receive points when the beeps occur. If the class is quiet for the 3 minutes, the yellow card is removed and all the students can begin earning points for being on task when the beep sounds.

FORMS

9.1 Signal Time Out Program: Teacher Designated Plan

9.2 Progress Summary

9.3 Signal Time Out Policy

Can be posted.

FORM 9.1

Signal Time Out Program:
Teacher Designated Plan

Target child: _____

Target disruptive behavior(s) _____

_____

Designated time period(s): _____

Baseline data across 5 days/sessions (designate frequency of disruptive behavior):

1. _____

2. _____

3. _____

4. _____

5. _____

Target goal (average or frequency of disruptive behavior across 5 sessions): _____

Signal time out mechanism (card, badge, sticker): _____

Signal time out period: _____

Criteria for adjusting standard up: _____

Criteria for adjusting standard down: _____

Reinforcement for reaching behavioral standard: _____

Who will implement plan: _____

Parental consent (if needed): _____

Administrator signature: _____

_____

FORM 9.2

Progress Summary

Date: _____

Child/Class: _____

Baseline rate of target behavior (mean percentage or frequency): _____

Current rate (mean percentage): _____

Progress toward objective:	Yes	No
Maintain current plan:	Yes	No
Revise current plan:	Yes	No

FORM 9.3

Signal Time Out Policy

You can earn points for being on-task, doing your work, or attending to me while I am teaching. However, if you engage in the following disruptive behaviors:

1.

2.

3.

4.

you will lose the opportunity to earn points for at least a ___ minute period. I will signal this by _____ . If you are quiet during this period, then, at the end, the _____ will be removed and you can begin earning points again for being on-task. If you do not follow the rules for time out, your time will be extended until you follow the rules. Remember, do your work—it pays off!

10

Removal Time Out for Severe Disruptive and Aggressive Behavior

BRIEF DESCRIPTION

Traditional time out (i.e., removal from area or class) is often used in an attempt to decrease disruptive and aggressive behavior. However, in many classrooms, time out may not be effective, particularly if the child sees it as a way to get out of doing class work. In spite of this possibility, when disruptive behaviors are of such a nature that the safety of the child or other children are of concern or the learning environment is disrupted to a substantial degree, the child's removal from the area may be a high priority. The removal time out program combines time out with an existing plan for rewarding appropriate behaviors in situations where the child needs to be removed.

Children receive points for being on-task during classroom instruction via the beeper system. If severe disruptive or aggressive behavior is exhibited, the child is removed from the area or class (see Form 10.1). During this removal time out period, the child does not receive points for being on-task as the beeps occur. The time-out period is specified in terms of a minimal amount of time the child is removed (e.g., 2 minutes). If the child continues being disruptive in the time out area, the time out length is extended until the child demonstrates she is ready to rejoin the class activity in an appropriate manner.

TERMS

severe disruptive behavior   behavior that creates a dangerous classroom situation or halts instruction to the class, in the judgment of the teacher.

APPARATUS

A time out area needs to be designated. This area should be void of materials or objects the child could use to entertain herself. In addition, the Removal Time Out Tracking Sheet (see Form 10.5 at the end of this chapter) should be posted near the time out area to keep track of each removal time out as well as the length of time the child remains in time out. In some cases, when dealing with extremely disruptive or aggressive behavior, a place that can be supervised by school personnel outside the classroom may have to be used. Site administrators should be brought into the design of this strategy.

BASELINE MEASUREMENT

A simple frequency count of severe disruptive behaviors needs to be taken for a 5- to 8-day period (see Form 10.4, the Baseline Frequency Chart, at the end of this chapter). The teacher wants to distinguish between severe disruptive behavior (which results in removal from area or class) and less severe disruptive behaviors that can be handled with techniques not requiring removal (see signal time out program in Chapter 9). More severe disruptive behaviors that could (or should) result in removal of the child are (1) attempted or actual physically aggressive behavior, (2) loud, verbally abusive behavior toward teacher or peers in the classroom, (3) property destruction, and (4) any other behaviors that create a dangerous situation or significantly halt instruction to the class (should be determined a priori).

PROCEDURES

1. Define the disruptive behaviors that constitute severely disruptive or aggressive behaviors (e.g., verbally abusive statements, profanity, aggression, tantruming, and refusal to return to seat).

2. Implement the beeper system for on-task behavior and collect baseline data on the rates of severe disruptive behaviors for the students being studied.

3. Specify minimum time out period.

4. When severe disruptive behavior occurs, guide the child to the time out area with no work.

5. Set the timer for the minimum period of time.

6. If the child continues to be disruptive in time out, do not release her when timer goes off.

7. Once the child calms down in the time out area, set the timer for a short time (e.g., 30 seconds).

8. If the child is quiet for that short time, release her back to class to begin work.

9. The child does not receive any points while in the removal time out.

10. The child can begin earning points once she returns to seat and begins work.

11. Another occurrence of severe disruptive behavior, no matter how soon after reentry to class, results in repeat of above process.

HOW IT WORKS

Removal time out is used for extreme disruptive behavior in the classroom, where its continuance either significantly hinders the learning environment or jeopardizes the physical safety of the target child, or other children, in the class. The removal from class preserves the safety and the learning environment for the rest of the class. By combining the removal time out procedure with a reinforcement plan for on-task performance (i.e., beeper system), this program increases the motivation of the child to want to stay in the activity. Otherwise, the child may not mind being removed from the activity or classroom. It is therefore *imperative* that the beeper system (or some strategy that rewards on-task or assignment completion) be used in conjunction with the removal time out program, to minimize the attractiveness of being removed from class activities.

ADDITIONAL CONSIDERATIONS

Additional Precautions

If the child demonstrates extreme dangerous behaviors (e.g., assaultive behaviors to other students or the teacher), additional precautions may need to be taken to implement this time out. Crisis management techniques are described in other material and may need to be invoked if the child's behavior reaches a level where the safety of the teacher or other students is a primary concern. If the child becomes assaultive during an escort to time out, this plan should be reevaluated by persons who are trained in applied behavior analysis.

◆ HYPOTHETICAL EXAMPLE

Removal Time Out for Verbal Abuse

Ms. Jones is concerned about her student Raul, who becomes extremely verbally abusive to other students and the teacher between zero and one time per day. During these episodes, he may not be able to settle down for some time and the classroom environment is disrupted. Ms. Jones decides to implement a 5-minute removal time out in conjunction with the beeper system for reinforcing on-task behavior. During this 5-minute period, Raul will miss at least one and possibly two to three beeps. When Raul becomes verbally abusive, Ms. Jones will take Raul to the time out area. Her aide will remain with him until he stays at least 5 minutes in the time out area and is quiet and calm for the last 2 minutes. The aide sets the timer when he is escorted to time out. When the time out period is over, he is brought back to the class to begin working on previously assigned work and then can receive points for being on-task when the beep sounds.

If Raul does not go to time out willingly, he does not earn points during the time he should have been placed in time out. Ms. Jones has been trained in crisis management techniques, and knows what to do should Raul become assaultive. Additionally, a behavior analyst will be consulted at that point for possible changes in the plan.

FORMS

10.1   Removal Time Out Policy

      Can be posted.

10.2   Removal Time Out Program: Teacher Designated Plan

10.3   Progress Summary

10.4   Baseline Frequency Chart

      Teacher enters date for each row; circles number each time a severe disruptive behavior occurs.

10.5   Removal Time Out Tracking Sheet

      To be filled out each time a student is removed to time out area; to be used as documentation for its use.

FORM 10.1

Removal Time Out Policy

If a student's behavior is serious enough to cause me to stop instruction, she or he will be removed to the time out area (or removed from the classroom) to preserve the learning experience of others in the classroom. When the student demonstrates that she or he is ready to return to the learning experience with the rest of the class by serving _____ minutes in time out and following the rules for time out
(1) _____ (2) _____ (3) _____ , she or he will be returned and can begin earning points.

Try to control your behavior by refraining from the following behaviors _____
_____ so I
don't have to step in. Everyone can learn self-control. Practice it each day.

FORM 10.2

Removal Time Out Program:
Teacher Designated Plan

Target children: _____

Reinforcement plan: Beeper system (see chapter 1 for details): _____

Severe disruptive behaviors that result in removal time out: _____

_____

Baseline data (sessions or days):

         1. _____

         2. _____

         3. _____

         4. _____

         5. _____

         Mean frequency _____

Target goal: _____

Removal time out plan: _____

Time out area (in class): _____

Time out area (out of class): _____

Time out period (minimum): _____

Rules for time out: _____

Quiet period required: Yes   No   How long: _____

Who will implement plan: _____

Parental consent (if needed): _____

Administrator signature: _____

_____

FORM 10.3

Progress Summary

Date: _____

Child/Class: _____

Baseline rate of target behavior (range and mean occurrence): _____

Current rate (range and mean occurrence): _____

Progress toward objective:	Yes	No
Maintain current plan:	Yes	No
Revise current plan:	Yes	No
Adjust density of beeps:	Yes	No
(indicate fewer or more)	_____	

FORM 10.4

Baseline Frequency Chart

Child:_____

Severe disruptive behaviors (list): _____

Date _____	1	2	3	4	5	6	7	8	9	10
Date _____	1	2	3	4	5	6	7	8	9	10
Date _____	1	2	3	4	5	6	7	8	9	10
Date _____	1	2	3	4	5	6	7	8	9	10
Date _____	1	2	3	4	5	6	7	8	9	10
Date _____	1	2	3	4	5	6	7	8	9	10
Date _____	1	2	3	4	5	6	7	8	9	10
Date _____	1	2	3	4	5	6	7	8	9	10

FORM 10.5

Removal Time Out Tracking Sheet

Week of _____

Date	Student	Time entered	Time released	Comments
1. _____	_____	_____	_____	_____
2. _____	_____	_____	_____	_____
3. _____	_____	_____	_____	_____
4. _____	_____	_____	_____	_____
5. _____	_____	_____	_____	_____
6. _____	_____	_____	_____	_____
7. _____	_____	_____	_____	_____
8. _____	_____	_____	_____	_____
9. _____	_____	_____	_____	_____
10. _____	_____	_____	_____	_____

Relaxation Training

BRIEF DESCRIPTION

Some children, when they get upset, escalate rapidly to violent, verbal, or physically aggressive behavior. While behavioral management techniques have been proven to be effective with these children in the long term, other techniques may be employed to reduce the anger in the short term. One such technique may be relaxation training (see Goldfried & Davison, 1976, for a detailed description). If the child can be taught to calm down when he is getting upset, the incident may not escalate to an emotional violent outburst.

To initiate this program, the child is taught how to relax. This initial relaxation training can be conducted by the teacher in a group or a school psychologist or guidance counselor individually. Obviously, they must be trained in relaxation techniques. Also, younger children may not be able to benefit from relaxation training. Once the child can relax on cue, he is taught to identify the conditions under which he gets upset and to immediately self-cue the relaxation response. Relaxation should be practiced periodically by the child at times when he is not upset to ensure his ability to cue relaxation during stressful times. This is an excellent technique for older students, especially when combined with other behavioral plans to increase performance.

APPARATUS

Relaxation training audiotapes are available that students can follow individually. If your school does not have such tapes, then the school psychologist, guidance counselor, or teacher will have to be competent in conducting relaxation training. An audiotape can be made of the first session, which the student can use outside of the therapy sessions.

RELAXATION METHOD

A technique that involves progressive muscular relaxation involves several components. The child is seated comfortably on a couch or recliner and then asked to visualize a pleasant scene. Once he appears relaxed, relaxation training is initiated. The student concentrates on tightening and relaxing each muscle group (called *contrast training*). A few of the muscle areas involved in relaxation are the forearms, biceps, forehead, shoulders, neck, chest, stomach, and buttocks.

The relaxation training initially cues the tensing and relaxing of each muscle area, and begins to teach the child how to determine if a given muscle area is tense or relaxed, on the basis of the contrast between tense and relaxed muscles. With this skill, the child can cue each muscle area to relax when needed.

It is advisable to consult Goldfried and Davison's (1976) chapter on relaxation training before conducting this training, as well as to receive training/supervision from a therapist skilled in relaxation training.

DETERMINING THE CHILD'S "STRESS TRIGGERS"

To effectively use the child's new-found ability to relax, the teacher/guidance counselor must identify what stressful situations seem to provoke or trigger the child to become emotional and upset. This can be done by observing the child over time as well as asking him. Once these triggers are identified, role-playing can be used to teach the child to relax instead of becoming angry during such situations. The child also can be taught to leave an "emotionally charged" situation, if feasible. Here are some questions to help identify the child's triggers:

- Under what circumstances does the child get upset or angry. What is said, what is done, what does the child do?
- Does the child get upset during classroom instruction, games, peer play, or recess/free time? What are the circumstances under which the child gets upset?

Epilogue

The material in this text provides the user with 11 practical classroom management plans for two common problem areas: (1) on-task behavior and assignment completion and (2) disruptive behavior and rule violations. Of course there are many more plans one could design, but these 11, and variations thereof, constitute a formidable arsenal of techniques for a teacher to use in the classroom.

Before closing, a few tips and suggestions are offered to the teacher:

1. *Approach the solving of behavior problems with confidence.* Armed with these plans, have the attitude that you can eventually solve a problem. Don't settle for defeat before you begin!

2. *Don't give up too easily.* It may take several variations of your first plan before you find the right combination of procedures. Develop a "don't quit" attitude.

3. *Let data be your guide.* Learn to rely on the analysis of the child's performance to guide your teaching and management strategies.

4. *Realize your importance.* You are often one of the major influences in a child's current and future life. Your role in society is of utmost importance. What you do today can make a difference.

5. *Keep up with the empirical base.* While some research in education may seem as if it has no relevance to everyday teaching (and may not), the material presented herein does have relevance and it is advanced on the basis of many studies. Consult the journals listed in the references for up-to-date information of effective techniques that have been validated through research findings.

6. *Be an advocate for effective techniques.* When you see ineffective techniques being used by others, serve as a resource.

References

Barrish, H. H., Saunders, M., & Wolf, M. M. (1969). Good behavior game: Effects of individual contingencies for group consequences on disruptive behavior in a classroom. *Journal of Applied Behavior Analysis, 2,* 119–124.

Bickel, W. E., & Bickel, D. D. (1986). Effective schools, classrooms, and instruction: Implications for special education. *Exceptional Children, 52,* 489–500.

Brophy, J., & Good, T. L. (1986). Teacher behavior and student achievement. In M. C. Wittrock (Ed.), *Handbook of research on teaching* (3rd ed., pp. 328–375). Upper Saddle River, NJ: Prentice Hall.

Cipani, E. (1990). The communicative function hypothesis: An operant behavior perspective. *Journal of Behavior Therapy and Experimental Psychiatry, 21,* 239–247.

Cipani, E. (1993). *Non-compliance: Four strategies that work.* Reston, VA: Council for Exceptional Children.

Cipani, E. (1994). Treating children's severe behavior disorders: A behavioral diagnostic system. *Journal of Behavior Therapy and Experimental Psychiatry, 25,* 293–300.

Cohen, M. E., & Close, D. W. (1975). Retarded adults' discrete work performance in a sheltered workshop as a function of overall productivity and motivation. *American Journal of Mental Deficiency, 79,* 426–529.

Dietz, S. M., & Repp, A. C. (1973). Decreasing classroom misbehavior through the use of DRL schedules of reinforcement. *Journal of Applied Behavior Analysis, 6,* 457–464.

Erken, N., & Henderson, H. (1989). *Practice skills mastery program.* Logan, UT: Mastery Programs Limited.

Foxx, R. M., & Shapiro, S. T. (1978). The time-out ribbon: A nonexclusionary timeout procedure. *Journal of Applied Behavior Analysis, 11,* 125–136.

Goldfried, M. R., Davison, G. C. (1976). *Clinical behavior therapy.* New York: Holt, Rinehart & Winston.

Harris, V. W., & Sherman, J. A. (1973). Use and analysis of the "good behavior game" to reduce disruptive classroom behavior. *Journal of Applied Behavior Analysis, 6,* 405–417.

Henderson, H. S., Jenson, W. R., Erken, N. R., Davidsmeyer, P. L., & Lampe, S. (1986). Variable interval reinforcement as a practical means of increasing and maintaining on-task behavior in classrooms. *Education and Treatment of Children, 9,* 250–263.

Homme, L., Csanyi, A., Gonzales, M. A., & Rechs, J. R. (1970). *How to use contingency contracting in the classroom.* Champaign, IL: Research Press.

Iwata, B. A. (1987). Negative reinforcement in applied behavior analysis: An emerging technology. *Journal of Applied Behavior Analysis, 20,* 361–378.

Iwata, B. A., Bailey, J. S., Brown, K. M., Foshee, T. J., & Alpert, M. (1976). A performance-based lottery to improve residential care and training by institutional staff. *Journal of Applied Behavior Analysis, 9,* 417–431.

Iwata, B. A., Vollmer, T. R., & Zarcone, J. H. (1990). The experimental (functional) analysis of behavior disorders: Methodology, applications, and limitations. In A. C. Repp & N. N. Singh (Eds.), *Current perspectives in nonaversive and aversive interventions with developmentally disabled persons* (pp. 301–330). Sycamore, IL: Sycamore Publishing Co.

Jackson, G. M. (1979). The use of visual orientation feedback to facilitate attention and task performance. *Mental Retardation, 27,* 281–304.

Kazdin, A. E., & Bootzin, R. R. (1972). The token economy: An evaluative review. *Journal of Applied Behavior Analysis, 5,* 343–372.

Kazdin, A. E., & Klock, J. (1973). The effects of nonverbal teacher approval on student attentive data. *Journal of Applied Behavior Analysis, 6,* 643–654.

Kerr, M. M., & Nelson, C. M. (1993). *Strategies for managing behavior problems in the classroom* (2nd ed.). Upper Saddle River, NJ: Merrill/Prentice Hall.

Madsen, C. H., Jr., Becker, W. C., & Thomas, D. R. (1968). Rules, praise, and ignoring: Elements of elementary classroom control. *Journal of Applied Behavior Analysis, 1,* 139–150.

McLaughlin, T. F. (1983). Effects of self-recording for on-task and academic responding: A long term analysis. *Journal for Special Education Technology, 5*(3), 5–12.

McLaughlin, T. F. (1984). A comparison of self-recording and self-recording plus consequences for on-task and assignment completion. *Contemporary Educational Psychology, 9,* 185–192.

Medland, M. B., & Stachnik, T. J. (1972). Good-behavior game: A replication and systematic analysis. *Journal of Applied Behavior Analysis, 5,* 45–51.

Narayan, J. S., Heward, W. L., Gardner, R., Courson, F. H., & Omness, C. K. (1990). Using response cards to increase student participants in an elementary classroom. *Journal of Applied Behavior Analysis, 23,* 483–490.

Premack, D. (1965). *Reinforcement theory.* In D. Levine (Ed.), Nebraska Symposium on Motivation. Lincoln, NE: University of Nebraska Press.

Repp, A. C., Barton, L. E., & Brulle, A. R. (1983). A comparison of two procedures for programming the differential reinforcement of the behaviors. *Journal of Applied Behavior Analysis, 16,* 435–445.

Salen, S. J., & Gordon, B. D. (1987). A group-oriented timeout ribbon procedure. *Behavioral Disorders, 12,* 131–137.

Schipp, S. L., Baker, R. J., & Cuvo, A. J. (1980). The relationship between attention to work task and production rate of a mentally retarded client. *Mental Retardation, 18,* 241–243.

Speltz, M. L., Wenters-Shimamaura, J., & McReynolds, W. T. (1982). Procedural variations in group contingencies: Effects on children's academic and social behaviors. *Journal of Applied Behavior Analysis, 15,* 533–544.

Walker, H. M., Hops, H., & Fiegenbaum, E. (1976). Deviant classroom behavior as a function of combinations of social and token reinforcement and cost contingency. *Behavior Therapy, 7,* 76–88.

Wolery, M., Bailey, D. B., Jr., & Sugai, G. M. (1988). *Effective teaching principles and procedures of applied behavior analysis with exceptional students.* Boston: Allyn & Bacon.

Yeager, C., & McLaughlin, T. F. (1995). The use of a time out ribbon and precision requests to improve child compliance in the classroom: A case study. *Child & Family Behavior Therapy, 17,* 1–9.

Zwald, L., & Gresham, F. (1982). Behavioral consultation in a secondary class: Using DRL to decrease negative verbal interactions. *The School Psychology Review, 11*(4), 428–432.